SG

ROBERT TODD

WALKING

MAINLINE

Sevengails Publishing

SG

Sevengails Publishing
PO Box 1276
Lompoc, CA 93438

First Sevengails Publishing hardcover edition January
2012

Manufactured in the United States of America

10 9 8 7 6 5 4 3 2 1

Library of Congress Control Number: 2011962321

ISBN 978-1-937977-00-9

Dedication:

To the officers, staff, and families, who went to work one day and never returned home alive.

To the correctional worker who comes to work on time, does the job, and goes home at the end of the shift. They who can leave their personal problems at the gate, do the job, and leave work at the gate on the way home.

To those who still walk the toughest beat in America!

To those who have completed their "Watch" retired or have gone on to bigger and better things.

To the wardens who made the job easy to do.

To the lieutenants who watched over the correctional officers.

To the training officers who kept us trained.

To those who responded to calls for assistance regardless of how they felt and put themselves in harm's way.

To those who have survived.

To Belinda Thomas who reviewed this book and provided her valuable insight.

WALKING MAINLINE

Contents

WALKING MAINLINE

WALKING

MAINLINE

WALKING MAINLINE

INTRODUCTION

It was Sunday, March 31, 1985 when I drove up to the front entrance speaker of the United States Penitentiary Lompoc California. The voice from the speaker went on to ask me the standard questions about contraband and the purpose of my visit. I informed the person on the other side of the speaker I was a new employee and was to report for my first day of duty on April 1st. He told me to go and park in the parking lot and report to the base of the Tower. I did as I was told.

The officer in the tower told me his name was "Jack" and he had me on the list of new employees after he asked me for my name and drivers license.

It was the first time I was reporting for duty as a correction officer for the Federal Bureau of Prisons also known as the BOP, a part of the United States Department of Justice.

Twenty one years later I drove away from that same tower and speaker on April 1st 2006, I retired as an active employee of the BOP.

In the spring of 2010 a friend of mine and I were attending a local festival, I introduced her to one of my retired co-workers from the penitentiary and his girl friend. As we talked about the events that had happened to us during our careers we both glanced at the two women, they had remarked we invented the stories we were discussing.

We told them we could not make up most of the stories or events that we were relating. Everything was true and there was so much more we did not have the time to talk about it all. Even my retired co-worker and I still cannot believe all the things that had happened when we worked at the prison.

If I was told I would work and retire from a career in the federal penitentiary, my comment would have been, "There is no way I could ever work in a federal prison."

Yet I started on "April Fools Day," 1985.

You pronounce the name of Lompoc as "lom-poke" like in cowpoke not "lom-pock." It is very common to mispronounce the name, but the locals will correct you fairly quickly.

I was wishing that each prison had a dedicated history department where the events of the prison could be researched. Photographs of riots, assaults, and escapes, would be kept there. A lessons learned place can be of extremely good use for staff training. This could save staff from getting injured or killed. At the least it would save staff from doing really embarrassing things.

I found in my career, the search log books of a unit would help me find where contraband was hidden in the past, and the places that would be used again by inmates. We had a staff member put together a really good reference book about the escapes and plots for escape at Lompoc. It was used in our training.

It took some time for many of the changes to be made that improved safety and security of the prison. One change from what you could call the good old days was the switch from metal silverware to plastic. It is more cost effective to wash and handle metal silverware, but inmates made some very good prison knifes from a metal dinner knife.

Tool control is very important. The best example is a simple hack saw blade. Even a broken one in the hands of an inmate is an escape tool. Common everyday items can be used as weapons.

It would be a nice thing to have all the experiences of retired staff and employees written down to learn from. This book is my attempt to tell the story of one prison, on how I did my time as a staff member, and was able to go home at the end of my watch.

"This is United States Penitentiary Lompoc, KOE956, Clear!"

WALKING MAINLINE

CHAPTER 1

INTERVIEW BOARD

One of the most often heard sayings after I started working for the bureau was, "I drove up to this place looking for a job and I will leave from this place looking for a job." I was looking for a job in federal law enforcement with a 20 year retirement program. The Federal Bureau of Prisons gave me the opportunity to have that job.

It is hard to believe a lot of people really like to work in the correctional environment and they enjoy working in a prison setting. My first thoughts about working corrections were why anyone would want to put up with the abuse of the job.

This was my opinion of an outsider with years of military law enforcement and investigator experience. It was a point of view of a non correctional worker, who wanted to see the criminal get convicted and put away. I did not care about feeding, housing, clothing, programs, education, and so on. Just put the bad guy's away, throw away the key, and no hug a thug.

My goal was looking for the great law enforcement job that I really wanted to do, and the FBI looked very good, but they had a long list of applicants.

The appointment to a federal law enforcement position had to be before that magic age of 35. At that time when you turned 35 years of age you were too old for an initial appointment in the federal law enforcement program. This was later changed to the age of 37.

WALKING MAINLINE

Applications had been made for several federal law enforcement positions. Those positions were for a treasury enforcement agent, a US postal inspector, a criminal investigator and others. The application and paperwork for correctional officer was turned in and a civil service pay rating of GS-6 on the general schedule of pay was the rating given by the United States Civil Service Commission.

It was about a month before my 35th birthday when a telephone call was received at work from a personnel officer with the Federal Bureau of Prisons. The question was asked if there was still interest in working for the United States Penitentiary at Lompoc California. The answer was yes, and it would have to happen pretty soon since I would be over the age limit in a couple of weeks.

Arrangements were made, the paperwork would be sent, and a courtesy interview would be scheduled at Leavenworth Kansas. The interview was not at the military prison but at the United States Penitentiary located in the town of Leavenworth. The question was asked where in the world was Lompoc?

The town of Lompoc is located 6 miles from Vandenberg Air Force base in California. The map shows Lompoc is 55 miles west of Santa Barbara at the dog leg of the central California coast. It was a small isolated city along the Pacific Coast Highway. Travelers from Los Angeles to San Francisco rarely drive through the city of Lompoc.

The drive to the US Penitentiary at Leavenworth Kansas for the interview was uneventful. The prison has stone walls and really looks cold and unforgiving. It is hot in the summer and cold in the winter. It looks like a prison. The center of the prison has a large distinctive silver in color dome.

Visitors drive up to the roadside speaker, the visitor is questioned about contraband and the reason for the visit. If you were there for an employment interview, you are told to park in the visitor parking lot and report to the base of the tower.

A prospective employee is told to go up the front steps of the prison, wait for the sound of a buzzer at the front door, open the door, go inside, and someone would meet them in the lobby.

It was just before 8:00 A.M.. In the front lobby I was greeted by "Fred" who told me he was the personnel officer. I was first for the board interview and there were two others to be interviewed. The interview would take about a half an hour and we would return to the front lobby. The board would finish interviews and we would wait for the results.

For the first portion of the board there were general questions about my background. I was told the interview would be conducted just as if I was going to be hired to work at Leavenworth. There was a reminder this was a courtesy interview for Lompoc.

Each member of the board asked questions about prison procedures and knowledge of anything about corrections. Each question was answered from what I knew about military corrections. The board asked a lot of questions on how things would be done.

Questions were asked about how to react in emergency situations. Questions were asked on how I would do things as a correctional officer. After what seemed to be a short time, the board announced it was time for a lunch break. It had been at least two hours of time being before the board. I was escorted to the front lobby where I could get lunch from the vending machines.

A few minutes into lunch the personnel officer came by and said I would get an escort to the medical department for a medical exam. He asked me if I was ready for the exam, I was. It was learned later if you were taken for the medical exam, you were hired to work for the bureau of prisons.

The escort was conducted by a staff member through the control center sally port to the inside of the large stone walled prison. A sally port is a controlled entrance into the prison where only one gate or door can be opened at a time to an area that is a room or passage that is like a trap. The idea is if an unauthorized person goes into this area they can be stopped and held. It is a controlled method of entry. The escort took me to the medical department.

On the way to the medical department which also housed the prison hospital, I talked to an inmate orderly who was operating a floor buffer. It was impressive how polished the floor of the hallway was.

I asked what kind of floor polish he used, the inmate told me no wax or polish was used. He had been polishing the floor for the past 20 years. The inmate asked if I was a replacement for the medical records clerk who had her throat cut in the hallway. I told him no.

The medical exam was a little poking and prodding. The doctor took blood pressure and asked general questions about any health problems. A plastic bottle was provided to urinate in.

The restroom contained a sink that had no faucet handles and a toilet. The goal was to fill the bottle to the line in a 2 hour time limit. Care had to be taken of not overflowing the bottle. The goal was met.

When escorted back to the front entrance lobby I saw a guy dressed in a gray work uniform with the largest set of prison keys I had ever seen. He had a key pouch on his right hip with what looked like two dozen prison keys stuffed in the leather pouch. The keys, were on a ring, clipped to a dog chain, and was attached to his belt.

When I returned to the control center gate, the officer behind the glass looked at me. He was holding his hands in front of his face, with his thumbs pointed together and the index fingers pointing upward, just like a movie director would do when he would be framing a movie shot. My escort told me that was the sign to show the officer my identification.

I asked the officer through the speaker which identification did he want to see, he answered my drivers license. The license was put up to the window and he opened the sally port gate. When I entered the sally port, he said to put my license in the window slot. He looked at it and slid it back and told me not to be a "Smart Ass."

I returned to the font lobby and was escorted into an office to fill out some papers. After that I was escorted out of the prison and I returned home.

A day or so later a telephone call was received asking if I was available to accept the job as a correctional officer at a

GS-6 salary of $16,575.00 per year. I was in federal civil service and this was a promotion. I was available and would accept the position. The papers were in the mail with a start date of April 1st at the United States Penitentiary Lompoc. There was less than two weeks to report to the new job.

CHAPTER 2

I DROVE UP TO THE FRONT

The drive out to Lompoc California was in a 1976 four door Plymouth Fury, it had a 6 cylinder engine, an automatic transmission, and rust on the rear fenders. The trunk was packed with clothes and some military uniforms for reserve duty.

The wife had served me with divorce papers, she said she wanted some space. I gave her 2000 miles of space. The trip was okay with snow flurries on the way through Salt Lake City, Utah. It was late in the month of March. I had gas money and about 200 dollars in my pocket. I did not have any valid credit cards.

The travel south of Salt Lake City was on the interstate highway. I ran into very heavy snow. The snow was falling so hard the windshield wipers almost could not clear the snow. The drive was up and down steep hills which had warning signs posted stating chains were required. You did not dare stop. If you did stop the car, it would be stuck on the side of the road.

It was just a little north of Saint George Utah when I had to stop for gas and use the rest room. The car top was cleaned off since it had over a foot of ice and snow piled on it.

During the fuel stop a truck driver pulled in and looked at the car with all the snow on it. He asked how bad the roads were. About that time a highway patrolman stopped

11

by and told us the interstate was being closed northbound to Salt Lake City.

Earlier in the trip a 4-wheel drive sheriff's vehicle spun out of control going up one of the interstate highway hill's, and since I could not stop to help, I just kept driving.

The truck driver said the road was clear about four or five miles south of town. After returning to the interstate, and after about five miles, there was a snow line across the road. After that it was dry and clear. I stopped at the very next rest area and fell asleep in the front seat of the car. It was very late at night.

The next morning I heard people talking outside the door of the car and I woke up and stepped out of the car. The car was covered with snow and ice! It was still about a foot thick and melting in the sun.

There was a sign that said "Welcome to Arizona," and I figured I had really gotten lost in the heavy snow. The rest area is in the north west corner of Arizona, just outside of Mesquite Nevada. The trip was continued into Las Vegas for a late breakfast.

It was midmorning when I arrived in Las Vegas. My first stop was at the Golden Nugget casino in the downtown area. It was also time to eat at McDonald's, then to try my luck on the slot machines at the Golden Nugget. I won $200.00 from a dollar slot machine. I quit playing the slots and it was time to leave Las Vegas for Lompoc.

A stop at the state line of Nevada south of Las Vegas was made at Whisky Pete's casino. After winning a $100.00 from the slot machines and a hot dog lunch it was time to leave.

The drive was through the hills of California to Santa Maria. The road was past Vandenberg Air Force Base and finally ending in Lompoc. It was Sunday afternoon. It seemed the town was out in the middle of nowhere. It took a while to find the penitentiary.

I drove up to the front entrance speaker. The voice began the questions about did I have contraband in my vehicle or on my person. The answer was no, I informed the officer I was a new employee and I was supposed to report to work the next day. I was told to park in the parking lot and report to the base of the tower.

I parked my car and walked to the base of the tower. An old guy leaned out the window and said his name was "Jack." He said to me welcome to U.S.P. Lompoc. He asked me for my identification. I ask which one, civilian, military, or what. He told me "Don't be a smart ass," and told me a driver's license would do, but it had to be a picture ID. He lowered a canvas bucket on a rope and told me to put my ID in the bucket. After a few minutes he lowered the bucket returning my ID.

"Jack" explained to me about reporting for work the next morning. He also said today was a visiting day. He asked me if I had a place to stay yet. I told him I just drove up and I did not have a place. He told me there were bachelor quarters on the reservation, but he recommended finding a place to stay in town. He then told me a guy at the prison camp named "Rob" was looking for a roommate to share a house with.

I asked where the prison camp was and Jack pointed out the window to his left. He said it was just over there about a half mile away. He directed me back down the road and around the corner. He told me to look for camp control and ask for "Rob."

"Jack" told me just before I left, when I reported for work the next day not to stop at the road speaker, and to park in the employee parking lot. I was to report to the base of his tower. He informed me someone from the training department would meet with the new employees.

I drove over to the federal prison camp. I did not know it was called "Club Fed" until I had worked at the penitentiary for about a month. I found the control room and the officer behind the desk asked "What in the hell did I want?", after I knocked on the window with black bars on it.

I told him I was a new employee and "Jack" from the tower had said "Rob" was looking for a roommate. Just then he got a phone call and motioned to stop talking. After he hung up the phone he got up from his desk and opened the door to his office and motioned to go on in.

He said if I had $200.00 for a deposit, I could move in but not until the next day. He told me he was working overtime and could not get keys to the house until after midnight.

That was all right with me and I would find a place to stay in town. He recommended I drive to Buellton or Solvang to stay. He said it was not that safe to stay in Lompoc.

We talked for a few minutes. He told me the house expense's and rent would be shared equally three ways and "Jim" was the other roommate.

He asked me if I had worked for the bureau before. The answer was no. I told him I just finished working as a civilian for the Army in a military intelligence unit. He said sarcastically that he was impressed. He then told me he had to shut down the office and leave since it was count time.

He gave me the address of the house and told me he would have an extra key after work the next day. He gave me the house phone number but said almost no one was home anyway to answer the telephone.

I left the prison camp and drove around the town of Lompoc and I found where the house was located. After a while I drove to Buellton, another town about 13 miles from Lompoc, found a motel, and spend the night.

The next morning I returned to the penitentiary, parked in the employee parking lot, and joined the line of staff going to work.

CHAPTER 3

INSTITUTIONAL FAMILIARIZATION (I.F.)

Every new employee at a BOP facility goes through the class called I.F. Every inmate goes through a similar class, but it is called admission and orientation, A&O for short. The bureau wants staff and inmates to know about their rights and responsibilities. The training is to show how the institution where they are going to live or work operates.

It was April 1st, 1985.

It was about 7:30 A.M. when I reported to the base of the front tower. I was wearing a blue blazer, maroon pattern tie, white shirt, gray slacks and black shoes. "Jack" was the officer working in the tower. He looked me over and said the maroon pattern tie was not authorized and I should go to K-Mart after work and purchase a clip on solid colored maroon tie. He told me to go on into the front lobby. I learned later there were about a dozen new employees in our I.F. class.

The rest of the class went through the process of putting their ID's in the canvas bucket so the tower officer could review and return them. Each I.F. class and new employee would have a memorandum about them in the tower, with the starting date of when they were reporting for duty. The tower officer was to make a positive identification of each new employee when they came to the tower before they could enter the institution.

I waited in the front lobby for the remainder of the class. At about 8:00 A.M. our training officer greeted us. He read off a list of names and told us to answer present when our name was called.

We had to sign in the visitor's log book. He then directed us to the metal detector we had to pass through without setting it off. I had to take off my shoes, my belt, empty my pockets and finally cleared the metal detector. He escorted us to a classroom on the second floor of the building.

Class started after we had taken the oath of office for federal employees, with each of us telling our names, a little about our background, if we were married, where we worked before, and anything else we thought would be important.

The training officer told us our I.F. class would be two weeks long. At the end of the class, depending on what department we worked, we would be working at our assignment until it was our time to go to Glynco, Georgia.

The staff training academy was located on the Federal Law Enforcement Training Center (FLETC), at Glynco, Georgia. Glynco is just outside of Brunswick.

We were told the academy was three weeks long. We were informed correctional officers would be working 26 positions, post assignments, and shifts in our first year of training. The Bureau of Prisons policy was all staff regardless of our job title, were correctional workers first, and everything else second.

In order to pass the course in Glynco, we had to pass the academic, self defense, and firearms training. According to our training officer in a lot of classes the majority of failures were in firearms training.

WALKING MAINLINE

We would have to pass our I.F. training before attending the academy. We were told the Federal Bureau of Prisons provided more training to its staff than any other agency. After looking back over my 21 year career with the Bureau of Prisons, that is pretty much a true statement.

In our class we had a medical record's technician, unit secretary, and the rest were correctional officers. Our training officer had told the class what a class breakdown would be if we stayed with the bureau for 20 years, most of us would retire as middle management. He said at least one would probably make warden, a couple would quit the bureau, and one might get an US Marshal's number.

Getting an US Marshal's number meant that you got arrested, convicted, and would be doing federal time, this would not be a good thing.

We were then given a form and told to write down our names. The first section was our legal name for signing checks. The second part of the form was for our duty names while working for the bureau of prisons.

We were told we would sign our official paper work with our first initial and last name. Our first initial and last name would be on our name tags and chits.

Chits were round metal tags that are used to account for keys, equipment, tools, weapons, and vehicles. The initial issue would be five. It took more than five to work some of the correctional posts.

We were issued a metal whistle. The whistle is an emergency signal device and not used very often. I did a really dumb thing one day and blew my whistle inside my car. My ears rang for hours afterward. Those were really loud whistles.

We were issued our I.F. class books. They were three ring binders, at least 4 inches thick, and there was a stack of paperwork we had to place into the binders. At first it seemed to me every policy for the bureau of prisons was in that book. I later learned how wrong I was!

The class book was just the tip of the iceberg for policy statements and how the bureau of prison's standards were supposed to be.

We had instructors from each department give a class to the new employees. If an instructor did not show up for a class, our training officer would take over that class. At the end of each module of instruction we were given a written test. We had many, many tests.

In the afternoon we had a security office give us a class on emergency procedures and how to draw our keys and equipment from control. The first few moments of the class was about emergency response of staff to calls for assistance.

We were told at the United States Penitentiary Lompoc every staff member on duty will respond for a call for assistance. The only exceptions were the tower officers, armed patrol officers, unit officers, and staff escorting inmates or visitors.

There were some staff who could not respond because of a medical condition, but that was rare. He then added a new hire would not respond until they were provided their identification cards.

Just after he started the class bells started ringing in the hallway of the administration building. They were called triple duce bells. He told us to stay in the classroom and he ran down the hallway and disappeared.

Other staff ran by the door, and it sounded like a herd of elephants with keys rattling from the belts. We sat in the classroom and waited to see what was going to happen next.

After what seemed like hours, in actual time maybe 10 minutes, our instructor returned to the classroom. He told us it was a call for assistance and two inmates had gotten into a fight. The instructor told us we could respond to such calls for assistance as many as three or four times a day.

The instructor explained in an emergency situation staff could call for assistance. One of the ways was to dial 222 on the telephone. This was called dialing "deuces." We were told it would be very embarrassing to accidentally dial a triple duce instead of another telephone number.

We were instructed when using a radio, we were to announce our post or location first before anything else. If an emergency call was being made and the transmission was cut off, the control room officer would at least have an idea where the emergency call for assistance came from.

Generally in my years of working inside the penitentiary, when a staff member called for assistance, it was about 14 seconds between the call for assistance to the time when staff were responding to the location where the assistance was needed.

Just think of it, how fast can a local police patrol car respond to an emergency call. When you are on the waiting end of the call, it seems that staff are taking their time to either have a party, set up a barbecue, or just taking their time, that time seems forever. In reality it is very fast.

It is also very stressful working in an environment where anything can happen and often does.

During the afternoon the class had talked about calls for assistance and having to respond. We had the question how many false alarms occurred? We were told as much as one third of the time, the call would be a false alarm. The best thing for an 8 hour shift of duty was boredom. Come to work, be ready for anything, go home, and hope nothing serious happens during the shift.

It was that first afternoon when we went to the personnel office for our official bureau of prisons federal law enforcement officer identification cards. We had our pictures taken, signed the cards, they were laminated and issued to us.

The identification card is considered part of our equipment and must be carried on our person anytime we are in a bureau facility.

Looking at the card is well kind of disappointing. It is plain, with a photo, signatures, and that is about it. Not much to the card at all. It is our "Get out of jail card."

When a control room officer asked us to identify ourselves or the tower office needed to identify us, this ID card was our key to pass the control point and through the sally port. If we forgot our ID card, there was a process in place for supervisory staff to identify the staff member so they could pass. It was always an embarrassment to that staff member. It was also a good lesson, don't forget your ID card.

Our training officer took us back into the classroom and told us now we did not have to stop at the road side speaker to obtain permission to park. We did not have to pass through the metal detector's to enter the institution. We now had to respond to calls for assistance.

During that first day the correctional officers in the class were informed by Wednesday we were to be in uniform. The proper correctional uniform was a white collared shirt, plain maroon tie, a clip-on was suggested, and gray slacks without pleats, black leather belt and black shoes. A navy blue sports jacket with the BOP seal would complete the uniform.

I was wearing everything except the plain maroon tie. We were issued a BOP seal for the jacket. We would be issued the plain black steel toe shoes from the laundry if we wanted them.

It was during this first week of training we were taken to the horror room. This was an area with two parts, with one part set up as a cell. In the cell was a dummy covered with a blanket lying down on a bunk bed. It was the actual dummy used in an escape attempt.

We were told not to count dummies when we did an inmate count. During the daytime the dummy looked like a dummy. During the night it looked more real. We were told if we count a dummy, we are the dummy. If we counted a dummy, expect bad things to happen to us. One of the worst things would be, we could be fired.

The other room had on display all types of contraband. There were prison knives, known as shanks, homemade tattoo guns, drug paraphernalia and other things found during routine cell and inmate searches. These searches were called shakedowns. The weapons that were on display were used during inmate assaults.

We learned how to conduct a full visual search of an inmate. This search is also called a strip search. This is the type of search when an inmate will strip naked and staff would conduct very close, visual, hands off search of an inmate. One of the less appealing aspects of the search is the bend over and spread the butt cheek's check. For a female inmate there is the added squat and cough portion of the search. The bureau policy was the same sex officer would conduct the visual search of an inmate.

COUNTS

During our I.F. class we were told the most important duty we would perform is inmate accountability. This duty is the counting of inmates and keeping track of them wherever they were.

The official count times during the work days were, 12:01 A.M., 3:15 A.M., 5:00 A.M., 4:00 P.M. and 10:00 P.M.. During weekends and holiday times, the count times would be 12:01 A.M., 3:15 A.M., 6:00 A.M., 4:00 P.M., 8:00 P.M. or sundown counts during daylight saving time, and 10:00 P.M..

Special counts and census counts would be conducted when necessary. A census count was more of an informal count.

The first count taken at 12:01 A.M. sets the count for the day. Any additions or subtractions to the inmate count are made from this count. It would start to make sense when we started working in the units as correctional officers.

Wednesday morning of the first week of training we were escorted into the institution of the United States Penitentiary Lompoc. It was explained the institution consisted of the housing units and the main corridor. The housing units were named, "B" unit, "C"unit, "D" unit, "E" unit, "F" unit, "H" unit, "I" unit, "J" unit, "K" unit, "L" unit, "M" unit and the hospital.

The prison was a telephone pole style prison with a main corridor measuring about 20 feet wide and 632 feet long. The front entrance of each unit would open into the main corridor. There was also a work corridor and gym corridor that lead to outside entrance doors.

We entered the control room sally port when the control room officer looked at each of our bureau ID cards. He had signaled to us by holding up both of his hands, thumbs pointing toward each other and the index fingers pointing upward, just like a movie director framing the movie shot. For the control room officers and tower officers this is the sign, "I need to see your ID card."

We entered the corridor and were escorted to "B" unit. The officer unlocked the front entrance door and we stood inside the door. Our escort explained to us "B" unit was the honor unit inside the penitentiary. The inmates had a door key to their assigned cell. This was because each cell did not have a toilet. The toilet's were in a common area next to the showers.

It was explained to us don't walk down the middle of the unit, walk under the tiers. If staff walked down the middle of the unit, inmates could drop things from the upper level. If an inmate dropped a mop bucket from the third tier, a staff member could be seriously injured.

The way the unit is set up is it can be an outer cell unit or an inside cell unit. The units were three stories high. Each story is called a tier. The walkway on each side of the tier is called a range for a range of cells.

Standing at the front of the unit facing the rear, the first floor range to the left is called "A" range, the range to the right is called "B" range. The next floor up, the second tier, the range in the left is "C" range, the one on the right is "D" range. The third floor or third tier the range on the left is "E" range, the one on the right is "F" range.

Cells from the front of the unit to the back of the unit are numbered starting with the number one and continue in sequence until the end of the range. For the most part each range had 20 or 21 cells. There would be one shower area for each tier. A cell could be as small as six feet by nine feet and seven feet tall. A unit could have as many as 120 cells.

We continued our tour to "D" and "E" units. These were dorm units. There were no cells in these units, just an open bay.

During the tour we experienced an inmate activity movement. A movement is a 10 minute time inmates may move from the housing units to various locations inside the prison without a pass. It is a time the main corridor would be filled with 400 to 500 inmates all moving from one location to another.

The first time staff experience this can be a real moment of panic. There is no separation of staff from inmates. All the staff were in with the crowd of inmates. I could relate to General Custer and what he might have felt when he was outnumbered by all the Indians at the battle of Little Big Horn.

We finished the tour by going out to the prison industries, mechanical services, and recreation yard. It was an eye opening experience of what it would be like just to get around inside the prison.

One key element to I.F. training was qualification with firearms. Most staff had to qualify with a revolver, shotgun, and the M-14 rifle. A few staff because of their duty assignment did not have to qualify with firearms.

The M-14 is a .308 caliber, semiautomatic, high power rifle. A good marksman can hit a man-sized target up to 1,000 yards away with this weapon.

We had a secretary in our class that maybe stood five foot tall and weighed 90 pounds. It was very hard for her to qualify with the M-14 rifle and the 12 gauge shotgun. The shotgun gave a bruise to her shoulder. She did qualify and did it without any pencil whipping.

We had a couple of times that class was interrupted because of a call for assistance, but most of our training in the classroom was uninterrupted.

WALKING MAINLINE

One of the things our training officer told us was Glynco would teach us bureau policy and when we worked at the institution we would implement policy on how things would work at the local level.

On the last day of I.F. I had travel orders for Glynco Georgia and would report that next Monday morning for the academy.

CHAPTER 4

GLYNCO

The departure from Santa Maria California airport for the Federal Law Enforcement Training Center (FLETC), Glynco, Georgia was early on a Sunday morning.

It was hard to imagine parking your car at an airport for three weeks and not having to pay for parking. This is what happened when I was sent to the staff training academy. Santa Maria did not charge for parking. That was a good thing.

It was a twin engine turboprop aircraft from Santa Maria to Los Angeles. Los Angeles to Atlanta GA it was in a big jet, then again in a twin engine turboprop to Brunswick, Georgia. From Atlanta to Brunswick it was a very rough flight through thunder storms and just really bad weather.

The arrival at the training center was almost a relief. It was after midnight. We were processed into the reception center and given an identification tag.

We were told not lose our ID tags. They were our meal ticket, room assignments, and our access pass to the training facility. It did not matter what agency you were with. Everyone had the same tag for wearing on the outside of our clothes. Many federal agencies train law enforcement staff at FLETC. It was interesting to see the other agencies work and undergoing training.

The lizard stompers were also known as the U.S. Border Patrol agents whose training started with exercises and running at 6:00 A.M. was an early morning wake up call.

29

WALKING MAINLINE

A van took us to each of our quarter's assignment. We were assigned two people to a room with a shared bath. I got to my room, turned on the lights and started to unpack at 2:30 A.M., early Monday morning.

My roommate woke up and asked who I was. He was an attorney from the Bureau of Prisons central office in Washington, D.C.. I told him I was sorry about waking him up, turned off the lights, and went to bed.

An alarm went off at just after 6 A.M.. My roommate was getting up, he asked me if I wanted a ride to breakfast. I told him no.

At 7:00 A.M. he returned to the room, I was still in bed and he said I would be late for class if I did not hurry. I told him not to worry, he said he was going to drive to the classroom and I could ride with him. I declined.

At 7:10 A.M. I got out of bed, dressed, and followed the directions I was given to the Bureau of Prisons training classroom. It was 7:25 A.M. when I took a front row seat.

At about 7:35 A.M. my roommate arrived at the classroom where the instructor told him he was late and to have a seat in the front row. Class started promptly at 7:30 A.M., Monday through Friday. My roommate was delayed in traffic. He asked me how I got to the classroom. I told him I walked.

Every day for the next three weeks I would stay in bed until 7:10 A.M. during the week and be in the classroom by 7:30 A.M.. My roommate would leave at 6:45 A.M. to get to class at 7:30 A.M. and he drove a car.

The training academy was not like a military boot camp. There was no yelling at the students by the instructors.

WALKING MAINLINE

There were no formations for class. Students were not tucked into bed at night and woke up in the early morning. BOP academy students were treated as adults and expected to behave as adults.

The instructors at the training academy said it was not a hard course, we had to pass the academic training, self defense, and firearms. If we failed any part of the training we would no longer be employed by the Bureau of Prisons and would be sent home. If we failed there would not be a second chance.

Every day of training we would have classroom instruction, fire arms, and self defense class. We would be given home work assignments and would have weekends off.

We were taken to a clothing issue point and given three sets of uniforms, white shirts, gray pants, maroon tie and our physical fitness uniform for training. We could purchase accessories at the store on the training center. There were about 30 students in our class.

When we returned to the classroom and were given a 3 ring binder, it was about 4 inches thick with a stack of policy statements. The policy statements had to be put in our binders. We also were given lesson plans to put in our folders.

After lunch it was on to the gym and the track. We were tested for how limber we were. We were timed on how fast and how far we could run. We were weighed in on medical scales, and did a weight lifting test.

WALKING MAINLINE

SELF DEFENSE

For the self defense class we would put on gym clothes, assemble in the gym to practice the bureau method of unarmed self defense based upon the martial art of Aikido. The terms most of the students will remember are, Ikkyo, Sankyo, and Kote Gaeshi.

Each of these are control moves. Ikkyo is a technique used to control the elbow and shoulder. Sankyo is a technique to put on a wrist lock. Kote Gaeshi is an arm bar technique.

These moves if applied right can control a very strong inmate. Of course so will a large number of staff responding to a call for assistance and that could control an inmate pretty well.

We were also told not to break our dummies, we would practice on our fellow class mates, and if we were too aggressive turn about was fair play.

We could "Tap Out," which meant if we were feeling pain or getting hurt. When we tapped out the classmate applying the technique would stop.

We had one girl in class really liked to inflict pain on her fellow students. She just would love to cause extreme discomfort to anyone she could. It got to the point no one would practice with her.

One day it decided enough was enough. She was placed in a very painful arm bar hold until she almost started to cry. She had tried to tap out several times. The arm bar was stopped and she was told the next time she injured a class member her arm would be ripped off and thrown in the lake that was on the training center. After that practice session she was getting along a lot better with the rest of the class.

In order to pass the self defense portion of the training, we had to demonstrate about a dozen moves, and techniques for our final exam. Each day we practiced for the exam.

We were also told that in the real prison environment we are to remember three rules:

Rule number one – survive, do what it takes to survive and not get hurt, expect in a knife fight, you will get cut, don't panic, and to stay calm.

Rule number two - survive to go home at the end of the shift.

Rule number three – write a good memo.

Many of the class really liked getting out the mats and the workout. Every year of employment all staff would attend annual refresher training. Self defense takes at least a half a day of the class. At times it seemed a waste of time.

The bureau would provide the training to say staff had been trained. In reality you did what it took to keep from getting hurt. You used what you could in a fight to survive then write the memo explaining what you did. You would take control of the situation and stop once the inmate was under control, or the threat had passed.

WALKING MAINLINE

FIREARMS

The BOP staff training academy taught firearms using three basic weapons, hand gun, carbine, and shotgun. Qualification was a must and not pencil whipped. We used a model 10 Smith and Wesson .38 caliber revolver. A couple of the class members had problems squeezing the triggers.

Red colored dummy guns would be issued to the student so they could practice pulling the trigger, build up the strength in the hands, and getting a good grip on the hand gun.

The first day of training three of us were pulled off to the side. The chief firearm's instructor informed us he knew we were good shooters. He knew we had shot in competition. He wanted us to try the BOP way. We were to use the front sights and follow the instructors training.

I made the statement and asked the question, "Was it not the idea to put the rounds into the "X" ring, since this was the center of the target? And did it matter how the bullets got there?" I was told "Don't be a smart ass."

When it was my turn at the range I asked if I could qualify on the first round and did I have to attend the rest of training. I was told I could qualify but I still had to attend training. The first day I qualified with the handgun, carbine, and shot gun. I passed the firearm's course.

One difference in the firearm's training was instead of starting at the longest range from the targets we started at the closest. This idea was to simulate an escaping inmate going away from the shooter. We started our course of fire at 21 feet. The full size target is quite large and close. It does not take much to draw and fire rounds into the target. We were allowed to load only five rounds in our revolvers.

We used a World War II .30 caliber carbine as the long arm. This is not the most powerful weapon to use. It was not like the penitentiary's .308 caliber M-14 rifle or later when the 5.56mm M-16 rifle was used. We were able to use two 15 round magazines with the carbines. The carbine reminded me of pop guns we played with as kids.

The last firearm used was the standard pump action 12 gauge shotgun. It was loaded with five rounds. We had to demonstrate, load the weapon, unload the weapon, reload, and then fire the five rounds.

If you did not hold the shotgun right, the recoil would bruise your shoulder really badly. The shotgun has a lot of recoil but it can be controlled. Street criminals and inmates showed a lot of respect for this weapon.

Every day was range day, after the shooting it was clean weapons time also.

CLASSROOM ACADEMICS

Sometimes the classes would be very, very long, dull and boring. We were told no sleeping in class. Sleeping on the job can be a firing offense. If during a class we felt sleepy, we could get up from our desk and stand in the back of the classroom to stay awake. There were a couple of times where half of our class was standing in the back of the room just to stay awake.

We were informed we could set up study groups and what areas we should study. Most of the classes covered the bureau policy and what was expected of the correctional worker.

We had at least one third of the class concerned about inmate discipline policy and knowing the incident codes. We studied for hours on this one policy statement. The codes were divided into 100, 200, 300, and 400 series.

The 100 levels were the most serious. The discipline policy was the administrative means for controlling inmate behavior. Violations of this policy resulted in sanctions being taken against the inmate. It was like the criminal and criminal court system. The 100 and 200 level violations would be like going to a district court for trial. The 300 and 400 level violations were for the lower court. Informal resolution was stressed. Not every incident had to be written up. We could attempt informal resolution of inmate behavior.

We were provided instruction how to write an incident report. Incident reports are also called "shots." This was the method of charging an inmate with a violation of the discipline policy. We were told the pen was the most important tool for controlling inmates. With a pen we could take away good time, place an inmate in the hole, and make life miserable for an inmate. We were to be truthful and document inmate behavior. We were also told and trained how to write good memorandums that would back up our incident reports.

We had training and films on how to behave if we became a hostage. The first rule was if we were taken hostage, we were no longer in charge or had any authority. We were told how to act during an assault so we would not be hurt or injured. We were also told never to wear clothing that looked like inmate clothing. We took part in a practical exercise where the class was taken hostage.

After the hostage exercise we had to write our memos. Once our memo's were completed and handed in we had extensive training on how to testify in federal court.

We then had a mock trial over the hostage taking incident. When it was my turn to testify I looked directly at the judge, said the greeting of the day, good morning or good afternoon your honor, looked at the prosecutor, nodded to him, made eye contact with the defense attorney, and since the "trial" was with the judge only, I directed my testimony to the judge. I would glance toward both attorneys from time to time.

As part of the courtroom exercise I had to read from my memo that I wrote. It dawned on me, after this classroom exercise, I wrote a really poor memo of the incident. The stress of the exercise demonstrated how difficult it was to write a good memo describing what had taken place.

During the critique of the class for the courtroom portion of our training it was pointed out I had done an excellent job of testifying in court. I sounded very creditable to the instructors. That comment made me feel really good.

We had a cell search exercise. Cell searches or "shakedowns" are an important and critical part of the running of an institution. During a shakedown the object of the exercise is to find weapons, drugs, and other contraband. The cell we were to search was a little larger than a standard cell. We were told to conduct our search in layers. The search would be divided into three layers, a top, middle and bottom.

The class was divided into teams of six people. We were given an hour to find the contraband in the cell. I would like to say our team found everything. We did not, it was embarrassing to be shown by the instructor what we missed.

It was a good learning experience. Later on during my career I had inmates brag to me what I had missed in conducting a search of their cells. As a matter of course I would go back to the cell and most of the time and try to find what the inmate had told me I had missed.

Role players are a large part of the training at Glynco. The role players are very good at their job. We were told they are contractors and work when needed.

Our class had an exercise that involved an inmate escape. We started the exercise with issue of the escape post equipment. This equipment consisted of flashlights, weapons, maps and our post orders.

Our class was divided up into teams. Our directions provided to us left us confused and it seemed like it was a real "Charlie Foxtrot." We were given conflicting instructions and it seemed so disorganized.

Our team went out and searched for the escaped inmates. The role players were really great! They acted just like the real public would. At one time our team leader had a "Suspect" down on the ground under gunpoint when the call came over the radio the exercise was over.

The team leader did not hear the call at all, he was so concentrated on what he thought was the escaped inmate that he did not pay attention to anyone at all. It took two instructors to get his attention and he finally heard the exercise was over.

During our after action review of the exercise the instructors were very kind to us. They told us we acted as real world as it would ever get, every thing that we had experienced, the confusion, the interaction with the role players, was just as it would happen during a real escape. Later I would learn all this was true.

The staff training academy is not that long at Glynco. It is over pretty quickly. A few members of a class fail the training. Maybe one or two fail the background check and their employment is terminated. Once in a while a BOP employee gets sent home before the class even starts. There are very few student recycles for the training.

For the final exam the class paired off with each other. One student would act as the training dummy. The other student would demonstrate the correct form for each self defense move on their dummy for the final testing.

It was during this exam I broke my dummy. It was one of the defensive moves that I took my classmate partner down to the mat. She got sick and vomited on the floor. She was out of commission.

One of the instructors replaced her so I could continue the exam. During the last required move, a takedown with a knife, I placed the instructor in an arm bar. He slipped on the way down to the mat and his shoulder popped very loudly. I released my hold immediately but the damage was done. I had broken two dummies and still passed the final exam.

WALKING MAINLINE

At our graduation ceremony we were given our diplomas and took our second oath of office for the United States Government. That oath was as a federal law enforcement officer. After the completion of the academy, students are returned to their various institutions for duty.

CHAPTER 5

ROOKIE YEAR

The Bureau of Prisons is a quasi military environment. The correctional department is even more so. You have a chain of command, uniforms, and the discipline of the military. You don't really have to adhere to the haircut policy but it is implied.

During the first year the goal is to work as many posts and shifts as possible. The term common sense is used many times. This term should be "common sense in a correctional environment." Some of this common sense is never go into an area that you don't have a key to or insure staff know you are in that area.

Staff members have been known to be locked inside an area they cannot communicate from or let other staff know that they are in the area. Most of the time at your house you do not lock the closet. In the prison environment you lock the closet, you lock your office door, you lock the bathroom door, and you control the access.

As a correctional officer you learn many things by just doing. Fellow staff members will let you know how things are run. Inmates will tell a new officer how things should be run. You listen and check out the information. You learn to be a good relief.

The best advice I was given was show up on time and do your job. This advice was given to me by an old time "Hack" who had years of working as a correctional officer.

WALKING MAINLINE

Showing up on time and being a good relief was critical. The common practice for correctional staff was to report for duty about 15 or 20 minutes early, report to the lieutenant, turn in your chits for the relief and go to your post.

If you were going to be late, it was good to call the person you were going to relieve and tell them what the situation was. That was called common sense, at least the staff member knew you are in route. If you were waiting for a relief and you called the person you were relieving so they would know help was on the way.

A few years later in my career a major overtime pay settlement was made to correctional staff for the hours worked reporting early for a shift.

I learned wearing the full uniform for me was a good thing. Having the coat and tie on all the time was a bother for some officers. For me I was able to carry my notes in the inside pocket, and the jacket would keep me warmer than not having one. Some post's called for nickel gray uniforms, these are a work utility uniform. Wearing the full uniform meant if an outside inmate escort trip was required, correctional staff in full uniform would most likely be chosen.

Having a clip-on tie also kept an inmate from grabbing the tie and choking the officer. If an inmate grabbed the clip-on tie, the tie would just break away. It was still assault on staff.

Dog chains are a must have. I know this would sound very strange to someone who does not have to carry prison keys for a long shift. A dog choke chain collar measuring 18 to 22 inches long, and is welded stainless steel, light but strong, is a must have.

You attached the key ring to one end of the dog chain by a snap link and the other end of the chain is attached to a belt clip. You need three belt clips, one for each end of the chain and the other for your chits. The chit holder is a key link with a screw on device you can put chits on and they can be secured so you don't lose the chits. The dog chain should be long enough that you can work the lock but not so long as to let the keys hit the floor when you drop them.

Years before I started work for the BOP, if a staff member dropped their keys it could be a firing offense. A few times it meant time off without pay. When I started, if by accident you dropped your keys, the question "Do you have kids and do you drop them?" was asked. It is pretty embarrassing to have the key chain clip malfunction and the keys hit the floor.

One of the rules was if you broke a key, you could not leave the key in the key way, you had to recover the key. You also were supposed to report the broken key so it could be replaced. You could not make your own copies of prison keys. Keys are a controlled item. Some sets of keys required a "Hot Slip," this was a document approved by the shift supervisor to have the key issued by control to that staff member.

A good flashlight is also a great tool to carry. Working an evening shift or morning shift and not having a working flashlight is bad. Even if you could use a flashlight from control or have one as part of the standard equipment, many times they did not work. A good two cell flashlight to carry on the belt and a smaller flashlight for the pocket is ideal. The professional law enforcement models are the best and having good batteries is critical.

Steel toe shoes, is another prison common sense item to wear. Steel toe shoes will help protect your toes if an inmate wants to stomp on them. They are a safety item when working. The one time you don't wear steel toe shoes or safety shoes is the time you get your toes hurt.

Being a new staff member and if you are a correctional officer just returning from the training academy your first assignment will probably be morning watch starting on Sunday. The work week starts on Sunday and ends on Saturday. There are several shifts for correctional staff, but for the most part the shifts are divided into watches.

Morning watch is from midnight to 8:00 A.M., day watch 8:00 A.M. to 4:00 P.M. and evening watch is from 4:00 P.M. to midnight. The other thing that was done between the hours of 6:00 P.M. and 6:00 A.M. were watch calls to control every half hour. The watch call is the time a staff member calls control to let control know all is well.

I was assigned to "C" unit morning watch. I reported to the operations lieutenant's office at about 11:30 P.M. for duty. I checked my mail box for any notes or assignment changes. I then went to the control room and asked what I needed for chits. The control room officer gave me the run down, body alarm, front door key, lock box key, office key, and I believe that was it. He also told me I should have more chits made so when I worked a post requiring more than the five chits we were issued I would not have to sign for idiot chits.

44

Idiot chits were the paper or plastic chits the staff member had to sign for from the lieutenant's office when the staff member forgot their chits or needed additional ones for work. I had a plastic flashlight and was told I needed to get a dog chain for the keys. I used my key pouch to carry the keys in, but did not get the lock box and front door keys until after 5:00 A.M. count cleared.

The corridor office let me into the unit and I spoke with the unit officer. He told me I was a good relief. He explained how to make the entries into the unit log book and showed me the post orders and the inmate housing card file. He told me what the base count was and I had inmate property to inventory.

He said the count slip was on the desk. He explained to me I had to count the unit and fill out the count slip for the 12:01 A.M. count. I would have to count the unit next door which was "B" unit. The corridor office will rack in another officer so we could conduct our double count of "C" unit and "B" unit. He wanted to see my flashlight and checked it to see it worked. He then left the unit.

I made the entry into the unit log book, the day's date, the time 12:01 A.M., all keys and equipment accounted for, and the base count of 120, the number of inmates currently assigned and in the unit. I opened up the post orders and started to read them.

As I sat at the desk, locked in a unit of 120 convicted federal felons, out numbered 120 to 1, and no other staff immediately available I wondered what the hell am I doing here?

WALKING MAINLINE

I was a Bureau of Prisons trained graduate of the academy and the I.F. course. I did not have a clue and was reading the post orders on how to do my job.

It was a surprise, when the corridor officer racked open the main door, that is he opened the door, and let a correctional officer into my unit. The officer informed me it was count time.

The main question was how do we conduct a count? He told me to get a piece of paper, start writing down the ranges on the left side in a column, A range through F range.

We would start on the third tier and count the inmates, making sure we were counting living breathing flesh and not any dummies. We were to start with cell number one on each range and proceed to count the inmates in the cell, using a flashlight to insure we were counting living flesh. At the end of each range we were to write down the total number of inmates in the cells for each range. When we returned to the head of the ranges, we would then compare the counts, if the numbers did not match, we would recount the range.

We counted each tier, added up all the numbers for a total unit count. The control room officer would double ring the unit when it was time to call in the count. A double ring was when the phone would ring but the ring would be like two short rings instead of the regular ring. Only the control room could double ring a unit. When you got a double ring in the unit, the officer was to call control as soon as he could.

During count times, the double ring would occur, the officer would call control and wait for control to acknowledge the call. The control room officer would announce "Control" the unit officer would state his unit location and say "I have a double count of 120," or what the count was. If the count was good, the control room officer would call out the name of the unit, and state, "That is a good count."

After the count was called in, the count slip would be filled out and signed by the two staff members making the count, then the count slip would be taken to control. Count slips and count forms could not contain any errors.

If the count was bad, control would tell the officer calling in the count, that the count was bad and to recount the unit. If there was a second bad count, additional staff would be sent to the unit to count. If the count was bad a second time, a picture book count would be conducted. This process was very disruptive but necessary to discover if there was in fact a missing or an escaped inmate.

If an officer had a history of bad counts, a pair of steel toe shoes would be nailed to the wall in the lieutenant's office or the officer's mail room with the officer's name on the boots. The toes would be cut out. This would be a clear message to the officer to get his counting duties in order.

During the day watch shift on a normal work day a twice a day unit census was conducted of the inmates in a housing unit. The custom was the unit officer would walk the unit and note in the housing unit locator book with a horizontal mark by each inmate's name that he was present during the morning census. A vertical mark would be made to indicate the inmate is present in the unit during the afternoon census. The inmate's name and number would be entered on the census sheet. The times of the unit census were 8:15 A.M. and 12:15 P.M..

At times a prison census count was made of all the inmates. This was an informal count of all the inmates in the prison. All inmates were counted in place and those inmates that were out of bounds were noted. This census count would be called into the control room. The paperwork would be sent to the control room also.

After the count was cleared by control, the main corridor officer came down to my unit and explained to me how to do property. An inmate that gets placed in detention also known as the hole has to have his personal property accounted for. If an inmate is released from the institution for an escorted trip, transfer, or other reasons, his personal property is inventoried by a staff member. The property is placed in storage for the inmate.

An inmate can file a tort claim for missing property that staff should have kept secure but did not. If the personal property is not properly secured and accounted for it can cost a lot of money to replace or reimburse the inmate for his property. I had two properties to inventory during that shift.

During morning watch and other times when there is not enough staff available to count, unit officers got moved around to cover the count. During some shifts an officer may count up to four units. The officers working a special housing unit stay in their unit for count and another officer was let into the unit to conduct the count.

WALKING MAINLINE

During the later portion of the shift for a morning watch officer in a unit it could get very busy.

When I started working in the prison each housing unit did not have electric cell doors. Some of the units had doors that required them to be keyed open by the staff member working the unit. Lock box keys would be passed out when the 5:00 A.M. count cleared. The front door key would also be issued. The crew kit containing 3x5 inmate photo cards for inmates assigned to the unit and pass books were also issued.

A crew kit is a pouch that contained an information card on the inmates assigned to work in the unit or who were to be in the unit during day watch hours. The inmate pass book was how inmates could be sent out of the unit during non movement times. A paper pass would be given to the inmate so he could travel from the unit to locations inside the prison. At the end of the day all the pass forms were to be accounted for. The unit had to be open and ready for business by the morning meal time, which started at 6:00 A.M..

During the morning meal times, the unit doors would be open, up to 400 to 500 inmates were in the corridor, and another 400 in the chow hall and maybe 200 in the gym or recreation yard. It was a busy time.

Officers had to make sure only inmates assigned to their living units were allowed in the unit. Inmates were not allowed to visit inside the unit unless that was their unit of assignment. This was sometimes a real problem. It would be during these movement times when assaults and killings could occur.

WALKING MAINLINE

If you had a good relief, an officer would report to his post or unit, chits would be exchanges, any problems noted and the shift officer would be relieved. When we were relieved from our post, it was still not time to go home.

It was the custom of correctional officers to gather outside the control room sally port and wait for the shift lieutenant to tell them to go home. If the shift was not filled, the officers would be asked to volunteer for working overtime at the post. If no volunteers, we would place a chit in a bucket. The lieutenant would draw a chit for an officer to work a double shift.

In the mid 1980's at U.S.P. Lompoc during some of the shifts, the whole shift of officers would have already worked a double and could not be made to work a mandatory overtime shift.

I had a good relief. I reported to the lieutenant's office and was told to go home. It was the end of the first day.

One of the things a rookie correctional officer looked forward to was being placed on the monthly rotation roster. The rookie roster was only good for two weeks at a time. It was designed to give an overview of the correctional posts available and the training to work the post.

There were times an officer who only worked a post for one day was training another new officer on how to work that post.

Being placed on the monthly roster happened because staff were needed to fill a post. If the shift lieutenant thought the officer would work out, the placement on the monthly roster would happen.

Generally after a year of working changing shifts, a correctional officer would be placed on the regular quarterly rotational roster. This was the goal of correctional officers. For 90 days you could look forward to having a regular shift and a job to perform, most of the time.

One good thing about staff shortages, a lot of overtime was available. The control room officer would call around to see if anyone "Wanted a hundred-dollar bill." This meant a 8 hour overtime shift.

An officer could add a great deal to his paycheck. Sometimes officers would compete with one another to see how many overtime shifts they could work in a two week pay period. The paychecks would be issued by our business office.

For a very long time I would work double shifts five days a week during my regular work week and only work a single shift of overtime during my days off.

During one three month period of time, an officer in our US Marshal's holdover unit was injured on the job and had workmen's comp time off. His shift was a 2:30 P.M. to 10:30 P.M. shift. I worked a 6:00 A.M. to 2:00 P.M. shift doing the early shift for the post. It was a hard shift to fill, and I requested if possible would I be allowed to cover the later shift. The assignment lieutenant loved the idea and so did I. I made a lot of overtime from that assignment.

One morning shift I reported for duty, the operations lieutenant informed me that I would be the segregation unit's (also known as the hole) officer in charge (O.I.C.). He informed me normally a rookie would not be in charge of the unit but he was short staff. I became a really good relief and reported to the unit early to find out what I had to do. I had worked lower "I" and the segregation recreation yard.

WALKING MAINLINE

The officer I was relieving said it was an easy job, I was told don't go down range with the O.I.C. keys. Count the unit and wait for an officer to be let into the unit for count, sign the paperwork on each inmate, feed the inmates in the morning, get recreation started, and if possible get the showers going for the day shift.

After a year, an officer, a good officer, could be selected for a promotion. In 1985 correctional officers started out at the civil service general schedule grade of GS-6, with a base salary of $15,497.00.

I was lucky, one day while reporting in for duty, there was an envelope in my mail box with paperwork stating I had been promoted to GS-07. The base salary at the time was $18,358.00 per year. A few weeks later we had a combined end of quarter party and promotion party.

It was during a morning watch shift after I had worked about six months at the prison the morning watch lieutenant visited me in the detention unit. He informed me that I and the control room officer were the two most senior officers on the shift. We were still rookies and only worked at the prison about six or seven months. We were just short of staff for custody.

CHAPTER 6

SENIOR OFFICER

After you complete the rookie year and if you are lucky a promotion to GS-7 Senior Officer can happen. You get a new name badge, blue in color, with your first initial, last name, and the title of Senior Officer engraved on it.

The officers at United States Penitentiary Lompoc got promoted fairly rapidly because of the staff shortage. A good work record and no negative 5x8 card entries by a supervisor meant promotion time. The minimum time in grade between promotions was one year. It was possible to get special act awards, a quality step increase in pay, or even just a suggestion award.

Depending on the warden, a monthly or quarterly staff recall would be held in our local staff training center. Staff members who were going to get an award were told to attend the recall. Really it was a meeting held in the afternoon, on a Friday at about 2:30 P.M. or so. After the recall most of the time was a tri-tip steak barbecue and a lot of beer.

At the end of each quarter for the custody staff who worked on a 90 day rotational schedule there would be an end of quarter parties. At least two weeks before the change of quarter, the supervisors, who generally held the rank of lieutenant, would change their assignments. This would give a supervisor time to learn the shift so they could have as few problems as possible for the shift change.

The goal of every correctional officer is to get on the quarterly roster in order to have a stable shift and regular days off. As a rookie officer the shift assignments would change along with the post assignment. Being on a quarterly roster, also meant that a lieutenant liked your work and wanted you to work for him.

Each quarter, shift lieutenants and the captain would hold a roster meeting. During the meeting each lieutenant would pick and choose whom they wanted on their shift. After that the correctional staff, who were not the best workers would be assigned to the remaining post assignments.

As a correctional officer you could put in for an assignment you wanted, but there was no guarantee that you would be assigned to that job.

I did not care where I was assigned. I liked working evening watch with Thursday and Friday off. That to me was an ideal assignment.

As a senior officer you are more independent and can train other new correctional officers. You could also be selected to be a "Peer Sponsor." The peer sponsor program was a program to help new staff adjust to the correctional environment and help them over the rough spots when they came up.

After you made senior officer, you could volunteer to be on special assignments, disturbance control, forced cell move teams, bus crew, armed escort, hospital duty, and other things having to do with custody.

I was selected to be an "Acting Chaplain." Being an "Acting" meant you performed the duty of the position but did not get the pay. You could be selected to be an "Acting Lieutenant," those assignments were normally reserved for a GS-8 Senior Officer Specialist.

WALKING MAINLINE

The religious department was short staff and one of the lieutenants thought I would make a good temporary chaplain. I had to escort outside civilian volunteers who provided the inmates with church services and insure the chapel operations went smoothly. I would assist the regular chaplain in his duties. It worked pretty well for a couple of weeks.

I was escorting into the penitentiary a rather sensitive group of outside visitors when I discovered they were attempting to smuggle narcotics into the prison. I seized the contraband, had it tested by the lieutenant's office and it tested positive for narcotics. I escorted the group back outside the prison and told them they could not return to the prison. I notified the lieutenant's office, called the chaplain that was in charge, then I had the inmates, who were in the chapel for that group's services returned to their units.

I had signed and distributed a memo to the front desk, visiting room, all the associate wardens and the warden's office on what had happened. I also went back to the chapel and told the inmate clerk the group was banned from coming into the prison since they were caught trying to bring in drugs. I talked with a couple of the inmate leaders of that group and told them what had happened. I was sorry for the problem, but drugs should be brought into the prison and especially into the chapel.

To say that I had caused a "Stink," could be an understatement. I was called by the warden to come to his office where he asked me what was going on. After I told him what had taken place, he requested that I draft a memo for his signature to ban that group from entering the prison until further notice. It was also a reminder to me that it was the warden who controlled who entered the prison. This was a major event and the warden had backed my actions.

It was later during my second year at U.S.P. Lompoc that a show down occurred between this same warden and the American Indians incarcerated in the prison concerning wearing of head bands in the chow hall. The warden had started a policy that no inmates could wear head gear in the chow hall. The exception was for the inmates working on the food line for sanitary reasons. The Indians wanted to wear head bands. The warden said no. The Indians threatened a disruption. The warden told them that would be a bad idea. The head gear band was still in effect when I retired.

During most of my second year at the prison I worked inside the penitentiary. I did not perform any duties at the federal prison camp. I worked a lot of overtime. I worked units, corridor officer, tower duty, segregation (the hole), and sometimes mechanical services to cover for staff during annual refresher training.

I had made the quarterly roster toward the end of my first year. I had a quarterly roster assignment! That did not mean a whole lot because we were roster adjusted almost daily.

We were still "Standing the Wall" at the end of each shift, and if the lieutenant could not find a volunteer to fill the position, the chits would go in the bucket, and if your name was drawn, you worked the shift. The good lieutenants would note on the 5x8 assignment card that the officer was involuntarily selected to work a shift. It was supposed to keep an officer from getting back to back selections.

There is a lot to learn working as a correctional officer. It seems just as soon as you get used to doing one thing it would change. Policy will change or a better way of doing the job came along.

During a late shift one day I was assigned as the work corridor officer. After work call was completed and the 4:00 P.M. count cleared the job of the work corridor officer would be busy releasing units for chow call, getting staff in and out of the segregation units, and working the corridor. The shift was from 2:00 P.M. to 10:30 P.M. or so. Just before the 4:00 P.M. count started I was called into the operations lieutenant's office. I was told to go relieve the "J" Joker unit officer.

I was told by the lieutenant he would get me a relief as soon as he could. I did not think much of it and went to relieve the officer. The unit officer had just locked down his unit. I informed him that he was to go to the lieutenant's office. He left.

It was not normal for the work corridor officer to work a unit. I was working the unit with a full set of corridor keys, the work corridor officer radio, the unit officer keys, unit body alarm, my flashlight and other equipment. This was a lot of equipment and keys to carry.

A second officer arrived to help cover the count. After a while the unit was called for the evening meal. The main corridor officer covered my work corridor post. This meant he was really busy.

The evening shift routine continued until the sundown count which started just after 8:00 P.M.. The main corridor officer racked two officers into the unit to help with the count. One of the officers had the chits for the unit officer I had relieved at 4:00 P.M., and he gave them to me. I was relieved of working the unit officer post and returned to my regular duties. I went to the operations lieutenant's office to let him know I had returned to my regular work. I inquired about the unit office I had relieved.

The operations lieutenant asked me if I noticed the small ice chest the officer had with him when I relieved him. I told the lieutenant yes I did see the chest. I was then informed the officer had the ice chest filled with marijuana, he refused a urinalysis test and was walked out of the prison. At the front gate I was told he was arrested and probably would not return to work. This information answered the question why I was sent to work the unit.

At least at U.S.P. Lompoc changes and suggestions were welcomed. If it made sense and did not violate policy you could do it. The suggestion would be written into local policy. It is what professional staff would do in a given situation that would be called sound correctional management unless you messed up really badly. The lesson's learned would be discussed in after action review's and would become policy. Policy was a guideline and not firmly fixed in stone.

Chapter 7

SENIOR OFFICER SPECIALIST (S.O.S)

Just after a year as a Senior Officer (GS-7) I went to the operations lieutenant's office at about 1:45 P.M., my shift for that day started at 2:30 P.M.. I checked my mail box in the assignment office and a lieutenant tapped me on the shoulder. He told me to follow him. He looked very serious and I wondered what I had done wrong. I was escorted to the captain's office. Inside the office was an associate warden, the captain, special investigative lieutenant, the operations lieutenant, and someone else I did not recognize. I was told I could stand.

The special investigator normally would read your rights to you if there was a criminal investigation, otherwise they could just start to ask questions. He asked me why was I late for my shift. I stood there for a second not knowing what to say. I then replied that my shift started at 2:30 P.M.. He responded in a harsh voice, "GS-8's report an hour early for their shift, or didn't you know that."

It took a second for me to collect my thoughts, the captain stepped forward, shook my hand and told me congratulations on being selected as a GS-8. I had made the highest grade for correctional officers! He then pinned on my new silver name tag. The special investigator then shook my hand told me he was happy to see the promotion.

The operations lieutenant then told me now I need to learn to work the control room. I reported for my shift. On the way to my post I asked the control room officer if he could help me learn to work control. He said yes.

WALKING MAINLINE

A senior officer specialist can work any post at any time. Most of the new GS-8 officers will take personal time to learn the control room.

The control room is the center for all operational activity in the prison. Control maintains the inmate count, unit assignments, key sets, emergency equipment, radio system, body alarms and other items to keep the institution operating. The control room officer is responsible for the operation of the grills in the corridor and the sally port. The control room officer is responsible to clearly identify anyone entering and leaving the prison.

After my shift that day I asked permission of the control room officer to watch him do his job. He allowed me to enter control through the sally port.

The first thing you notice in the control room is the key cabinet. The key cabinet stands more than six feet tall, three feet wide, two feet deep and holds more than 600 sets of prison key rings. All the keys are numbered and some of them are restricted on who can draw them.

The most important duties of the control room officers are; count, keeping the inmates inside, insuring emergency response, inmate accountability, key control, and insuring only authorized personnel enter or leave the prison.

I spent more than 40 hours of my own time going into the control room to learn the different systems and how each shift worked. I learned how to issue the many keys and equipment needed for staff to perform their jobs. Each shift required a completely different mind set and things that had to be done. The day shift was the busiest shift of them all.

WALKING MAINLINE

A control room officer has to do everything all at once, listen for calls for assistance, fence alarms, normal radio calls, intercom calls, making announcements over the public address system, key issue, allowing access to restricted areas, and allowing people to go in and out of the institution without letting an inmate out that should not be leaving. An escaping inmate is not good for the prison.

The control room officer needs to be an expert on the rules, regulations, and emergency procedures. After normal working hours the control room officer is the telephone operator for the prison.

The radio call sign for the penitentiary is KOE956. The control room officer would announce after a good count, "This is the United States penitentiary Lompoc, we have a clear institutional count at 4:00 P.M. or what count time it was, KOE956 clear."

Other calls would be made by the control room officers, such as calls for assistance or just routine radio traffic. I was one of the few control room officers that was a Federal Communications Commission licensed radio operator.

The control room officer had a computer terminal that was connected to the main frame computer that contains all the selected inmate information. The system was called SENTRY.

The control room officer should be an expert in retrieving and printing rosters of inmate information for the various needs of the correctional services department.

The control room maintains a master crew kit card on each inmate and staff information cards. The control room also maintains the work site crew kit cards of each inmate work assignment.

61

WALKING MAINLINE

Most of the time at the penitentiary only one control room officer was on duty. At peak times at the start of the day shift and the end of the day shift a second officer would help the control room officer issue or turn in keys.

One of the worst things a staff member can do to a control room officer is knocking on the sally port gate to try to get the control room officer to hurry and open the gate. Unless it is an extreme emergency, the control room officer has to put a priority on what work has to get done first. Besides all the other duties the control room officers' main duty is to maintain the count and the control room log. Between 6:00 P.M. and 6:00 A.M. the control room officer maintains the watch call log of all staff on duty.

Most control room officers maintained his or her own control room book. The book is the guide the officer will use to work the shift. The control room book will contain examples of SENTRY rosters and samples of computer transactions needed for the shift. Post orders, notes, and other helpful information are also kept in the book. A lot of the time when a control room officer leaves his assignment for good, they will take the book with them.

There are a few times things can be very slow in control. That is a good time for the control room officer to review the emergency plans and to clean the control room.

I used to mop and wax the control room floor. I did the military method of using paste wax. I would set the wax on fire in the can to melt it, and spread the wax on the floor of the control room. This would make it easy to buff the floor.

One of the operations lieutenants almost had a heart attack when I was doing the burning paste wax procedure and I did stop it. I still waxed and buffed the control room floor during slow times. The floor was so polished it looked like water was on the floor.

A control room officer had to be extremely aware of everything going on in the institution and always watch the sally port and main corridor activities. Most of the time, the shift will go by really fast.

The custom was when the shift was over for the control room officer, he would stay for the count to clear, depending on what the officer's next assignment was.

Most of the time control room officers generally would have the paperwork completed for the current shift and would start the paperwork for the next shift. The log books would be completed and shift briefing would be completed. This would help the relief so he could be ready to work.

The next most important post assignments would be the access point assignment. Examples of those would be the front entrance tower, rear sally port, or other means of access to the institution such as through the bus gate. After that would be a main corridor officer, the officer in charge position in a lock down unit and tool control room officer.

The senior officer specialist was for a time changed to a senior officer supervisor GS-9, not quite a lieutenant but a higher grade than a regular GS-8. That program lasted for a short time.

Most of the time if you wanted a promotion to the next level, this being a GS-9 lieutenant, the officer put in for a transfer to another institution. You were supposed to be a GS-8 Senior Officer Specialist for at least a year before that promotion.

WALKING MAINLINE

Becoming a first line supervisor was a goal for a lot of the correctional officers. A few officers decided rather than be a correctional supervisor, they would become a correctional counselor. Being a correctional counselor means you became a uniformed member of the unit team.

Correctional counselors are assigned to a unit up to three years on a rotational basis. The counselor is responsible for all the inmate work assignments, unit quarter's assignments, and is part of the inmate team review. They have the most contact with inmates in the unit.

A unit team consisted of an assigned counselor, case manager, secretary, and the unit manager. Each team could be assigned up to 200 inmates. If an inmate was placed in detention, the correctional counselor would make rounds to visit each of the inmates on a regular basis. The correctional counselor would be part of the unit disciplinary team.

A senior officer specialist could also be assigned to be an acting lieutenant, officer in charge on outside escort trips, and other assignments requiring experienced correctional staff. They could also be qualified as instructors.

At the majority of Bureau of Prison institutions it took many years to become a senior officer specialist. At institutions where there were staff shortages, a good correctional officer could become a GS-8 officer in as little as three years. At other institutions it would take 10 to 12 years to gain the promotion.

As a senior officer specialist I did not want to be an acting lieutenant, I wanted to be a lieutenant. I took roster assignments as they came. I worked as the control room officer first on the morning shift, then the day shift, and finally the evening shift. I was assigned the post of control room officer for almost three years.

I did have other roster assignments, but as a senior officer specialist that assignment could change daily depending where you were needed. I worked as officer in charge of the special housing, the Cuban unit, the federal prison camp and was for a time the officer in charge of the Vandenberg Air Force inmate work crew. I was the main corridor officer and a trainer of other correctional officers.

I had the unique assignment of justifying additional correctional staffing for the units, the federal prison camp and attempting to get a number two control room officer post assignment. I had obtained about 90 per cent of that goal.

I was also assigned as acting industries lieutenant and the tool room officer. The tool room officer is responsible for issue, turn in, inventory, and accountability of tools in the prison. The tool room officer worked for the captain.

Armed Escort Training was completed. This is an advanced level of training for the escort of inmates outside of the institution. During the training there is extensive firearm training and training in the use of deadly force. Once you pass this training the firearms qualification becomes harder, during annual refresher training a different and more difficult course of fire is used for the yearly qualification.

Chapter 8

CORRECTIONAL COUNSELOR

One day just before my evening shift I was called into the associate warden's office when I reported to work. I reported to him and introduced myself. He said he did not know me but was told I did good work. He congratulated me on the selection as a correctional counselor GS-09 at the penitentiary. He said my unit and reporting date was going to be worked out. He also said personnel would have my orange colored name tag.

The orange colored "Squashed Pumpkin" was the nickname of a correctional counselor's name tag. Correctional counselors wear the correctional officer's uniform and are assigned to a unit team. They were not on the correctional services roster or part of the correctional complement.

The duties of a correctional counselor are many. They are the single point of focus for inmate care, work assignments, cell assignments, visiting list, telephone list and a whole bunch of other work involved with the management of inmates.

A correctional counselor walks the tiers without a body alarm, at one time without a radio, and carried just a set of keys. The case load could go up to 250 inmates. A few times a counselor may work a custody post but it is not that often. Most of the time I wore the complete correctional officer's uniform including the jacket. The daily work notes were carried in the jacket pocket.

WALKING MAINLINE

The correctional counselor sits in on the inmate team meetings. An inmate team meeting is when the inmate's central file is reviewed, progress reports, work reports, release plans, and other management data is discussed with the inmate.

If there is an assault or killing in a unit, the correctional counselor sets up the mass interviews of the inmates. The mass interview is just a screening interview of inmates for witnesses and information.

A good correctional counselor knows his inmates. A counselor is required to make regular rounds to the detention units, inmate work assignments, and to visit with their case load. Correctional counselors maintain the inmate visiting list. The counselor also is a member of the unit disciplinary committee, and can act as a staff representative before the Disciplinary Hearing Officer (D.H.O.). The D.H.O. is like a judge in court.

Correctional counselors conduct intake screenings of newly committed inmates, perform unit team assignments, conduct admission and orientation training, and are involved in inmate release plans.

A correctional counselor undergoes a lot of training during the first year of the assignment. The counselor has to be certified in the inmate disciplinary policy, central inmate monitoring, suicide prevention, small group leadership and other areas. It is good to be cross trained in other areas of the correctional field.

Counselors generally work day and evening shifts and get special pay for Sunday's and holidays. The job is a five day a week position. A counselor may work custody posts on overtime when needed.

I was quite happy on the selection. I went to the assignment office to check my mail box for the daily information and pick up any mail. I was ordered to report to the Special Investigative Supervisors office right away.

When I reported to the S.I.S., I was told I was being placed on home duty status. I was to call into the office twice a day at 8:00 A.M. and again at 3:00 P.M. for watch calls. I was to be available during the day for any and all telephone calls. If I wanted to consult an attorney I could do so at my own expense and would have to take annual leave to do so.

I asked what this was about and was told it was an investigation about my activities with another correctional officer I had worked with. I was ordered to report immediately to the hospital administrator for a urine drug test. I took the test and went home.

At that time the internet was not a common reality. Using dial-up sites with a telephone modem was the only way to research on line. After my duty day was over, I would download the federal personnel rules and information pertaining to federal civil service.

I was called into the prison for an interview with the special investigative lieutenant. As I was waiting at the control room sally port for an escort to the S.I.S. office, I overheard an associate warden tell two other staff members how he was going to nail a staff member to the wall. The associate warden was talking about me. One of the staff had tried to tell the associate warden I was standing behind him and overheard his conversation.

During the interview I was told the investigation was about a drug raid that was conducted at a correctional officer's house. I knew the officer and he was a good friend and co-worker.

It was a few days earlier after work I had stopped by his place only to discover his house had been broken into. The door had been knocked off its hinges. I was about to contact the local police when a neighbor told me that there was a drug raid conducted at the house earlier in the day. I went home to get my camera and returned to take photos of the inside of the house and garage. The place was a real mess!

Later that day I met with my friend's father who was bailing his son out of jail. I talked with my friend after he was released. He showed me a search warrant and the supporting affidavit that went with the warrant.

The paperwork indicated he was running a meth lab and was a drug dealer. The affidavit stated there were comings and goings at all hours of the day and night by motorcycle riders and he was selling drugs from his house and garage.

The paperwork had written in it he had two 55 gallon barrels blue in color that contained drug making apparatus. He also had over a half dozen 5 gallon buckets with drug precursor chemicals in them for the manufacture of drugs. The paperwork also indicated a pipe bomb was found in the living room of the house.

The officers who found the bomb had placed the device in the center of the living room on a sofa cushion and continued to conduct the search of the house. The search team worked around the bomb. No actual drugs were found in the search or at least anything that could be credited to him.

WALKING MAINLINE

I was intimately familiar with my friend's house and garage. Several of us would ride our motorcycles over to his place at all hours of the day, after shifts were completed to work on cars, my pickup, and his Volkswagen in the garage. We would have barbecue's and beer in the back yard and in the garage.

The blue 55 gallon plastic containers described in the search warrant affidavit contained engine parts. One of the containers had all the engine parts from my pickup in it. It was an easy storage solution.

The 5 gallon containers held the used oil from the cars and trucks when we did oil changes. It is illegal in California to dump used oil. We would fill the buckets with used engine oil and wait for the twice a year roundup the city of Lompoc would conduct to dispose of the oil.

The pipe bomb had me stumped for a while. I was over at the garage a day or two later when my friend showed me road flares that had been unwrapped and left on the workbench in the garage. I looked over my photographs and saw the same road flares unwrapped and torn apart laying by the containers. My friend told me he found the flares on the floor and could not figure out why someone would unwrap them. He had put them on the work bench. I told him from the photos I had taken, maybe that was what the pipe bomb was all about.

We both wondered if a bomb was found at his house, why would it be moved, put on sofa cushions in the middle of the living room, and why the officers would be working around it. In my dealings with explosive devices if one was found, you cleared the area, and got the bomb disposal experts to come take care of the device.

71

WALKING MAINLINE

Since it was my day off, I went to the county district attorney's office to report what I knew of the raid. I took a copy of my photographs and provided an affidavit about what was in the photos, my friend's house, and in his garage.

There are at least two sections of the United States Criminal Code that compelled me to report what I knew of the incident. Title 18 of the United States Code, section 4 misprision of felony, and section 3, accessory after the fact, were the main parts of the law that applied in this case. My concern was any evidence collected was false, or even if the case was taken to court, all of it was based upon false information in a boiler plate affidavit.

The end result of this was the State of California did not file a case against my friend and co-worker. Later a federal case was filed.

While I was on home duty status I prepared a 35 page affidavit and a letter to the warden explaining what the facts as I knew they were. I included photographs that I had taken of the scene after the raid. I mailed the letter package to him at the prison, certified mail with a return receipt.

About a week after I had mailed the letter, I received a telephone call from the assignment office. I was asked if I could report to work that day for a 2:00 P.M. to 10:00 P.M. shift. I told the officer I would be there.

When I returned to work, I visited the associate warden who had said he wanted to nail me to the wall. I told him to give me a memo signed by him telling me not to take the actions that I did as required by law. I told him as soon as he signed the memo and gave it to me one of my last acts as a bureau of a prison employee would be to have him indicted by a federal grand jury for obstruction of justice, and get him a United States Marshal number. An obstruction of justice conviction can get a lot of federal prison time.

A short time after I returned to work, I was told to report to the "J" unit team for my first assignment as a correctional counselor. At that time, "J" unit, known as Joker unit, was our UNICOR unit. The inmates assigned to the unit worked in our prison factories.

After my assignment to the unit I was later told I had been selected as a GS-9 Lieutenant at two other institutions. The warden said he wanted me as a counselor at U.S.P. Lompoc and that is what I was going to do because he liked my work. All I cared I was promoted to GS-9 and got the pay for the job.

The unit counselor was generally the person who would set up the mass interview teams in a unit if an incident happened in the unit. Incidents such as assault, escape, killing, riot or other disturbance would require mass inmate interviews. Teams would consist of two members with escort staff who would bring the inmates from the housing cell to the interview team. The interview would consist of obtaining the name, register number, cell assignment, and work assignment of the inmate.

The interview would only take about five minutes and was more or less a screening interview. If an inmate did not want to cooperate with the basic questions he could be held for a longer time in the interview area.

This longer time could result in other inmates thinking the inmate was being a "Snitch" when in fact they were not. If a witness for the incident was found, a later follow up interview would be conducted. The mass interview was also an opportunity to see if any other inmates were involved in an incident and to check for injuries.

I would maintain what I called a unit information book. It could also be referred as a unit intelligence book. It was a 3 ring binder I kept an inmate crew kit card photo in a plastic sheet used for keeping photographic slides in. I could get 12 photos on a sheet. The case load varied from 160 to 190 inmates for a unit and I used 16 sheets in the binder.

The photo's made it easy to make an enlargement on the copy machine to use during a mass interview. A lot of the time inmates may not know the name of the inmate victim, but knew the inmate from a photograph and could provide the nickname of the inmate.

When interview teams were formed it made it an easy matter to take the photo from the book rather than having to hunt down the inmate central file. The next section of the information book I maintained a summary printout of the inmate's basic data that was available from SENTRY.

I had a summary printout of any disciplinary reports, designation information, and some other information. In three or four pages pretty much all the information that was needed to deal with an inmate was in one handy place. I had a unit roster with the inmate name, register number, work assignment, and any other information I thought was needed. I had a nickname listing since sometimes it was a lot easier to find out things about an inmate by his nick name than by any other means. I had an associate list of inmates and who they hung out or were associated with.

WALKING MAINLINE

Quite a few times when an incident occurred in the unit, just reviewing the book could give all the information needed to solve the case. The book was a very useful tool to use in providing information to our special investigative department or agencies like the FBI.

I maintained a working file folder on every inmate on my case load. These were copies of the forms that I had an inmate fill out when he arrived in the unit. Visiting list forms, telephone list forms, UNICOR or prison industries job application, and any notes that were needed in order to do the job as a correctional counselor. The original documentation was filed in the inmate's central file.

A few times an inmate would complain a visitor was not his list or some other thing was not being done for him. With this working file it could be shown the inmate did not make the request for what he claimed was not being done for him. The working files were a very useful tool and did not take much work to maintain.

I carried over my habit of taking notes on letter size envelopes. I would make notes on the envelope when an inmate made a request and I would file the information or take action by using the notes as a reminder. For me it was a very good system. The cost of an envelope was not very much, and I could carry the envelope in my jacket pocket.

I wore the regular correctional officer uniform consisting of a blue blazer, white shirt, maroon colored tie, gray slacks and black steel toe shoes. I had the stainless steel dog chain with a snap ring on one end and belt key keepers for my set of prison keys. Most of the time when I was in full uniform I avoided quite a few of the work details that were handed out from time to time.

WALKING MAINLINE

One of the time-consuming duties of a correctional counselor was to provide telephone calls to inmates on the unit team telephone. Policy allowed the unit manager to approve a 15 minute telephone call to an inmate.

The illusion to the inmates was I provided free telephone calls to inmates just about anytime they wanted. The fact was an inmate would apply for a monitored telephone call on a form to the unit manager. Only about one third of the inmate requests were approved. I would maintain the forms until the inmate got his call, then the form was filed in his central file.

An inmate could request an unmonitored legal telephone call. The unit correctional counselor would verify the call was to an attorney or other authorized individual and set up an appointment for the telephone call. Only about four or five calls an hour could be made.

There was a provision for a short three minute telephone call, called a "Fish Call" for an inmate to make if he just arrived. The "Fish Call" was to provide the family of the inmate information when the inmate arrived and the address to send mail to him.

One of the other policy requirements was a correctional counselor would have to visit the work site of each inmate on the case load. The counselor had to make rounds of the inmates that were placed in the "Hole."

I had a complaint one time that I was not making the segregation rounds. The inmates on my case load that were placed in the "Hole" saw me three to four times a week. I began the practice of having the inmates initial on the SENTRY assignment roster next to their name when I visited them. The complaint went away. I used the roster as a tool to track the requests of the inmates who were locked up so I could help them with the request. The roster was a real time saving tool that would prove very useful in the management of inmates on the case load.

One day I had an inmate come into my office during an open door time and tell me he should have been released over a month ago. Like most things inmates say I told him I would check it out. It was later that day I checked with our record's department to find out what his release date was supposed to be. The staff member who was in charge of the inmate's sentence computation told me he would get to it later.

I was not satisfied with that answer. I contacted the head of the department. The inmate's records were checked and it was determined his release date was almost 45 days past due. It was a rush to get all the paperwork in motion and to get the inmate released. It was after the 4:00 P.M. count that cleared that day, when I picked the inmate up in the unit, escorted him to our receiving and discharge department. He was issued street clothing and given his gate money. I then met him outside of the prison gate and told him "Don't come back!" The bureau paid for his extra time he was in prison.

The unit team's used to have a sliding glass door to the offices. My unit was "L" Lincoln unit and I had my office on the second floor of the unit. One evening an inmate came into the waiting area of the team office and threw a chair into the safety glass, shattering the glass door and window. It sounded like a shotgun blast. My desk was covered with broken glass, I dialed "222" triple duce's for assistance.

WALKING MAINLINE

Staff arrived responding to the call for assistance, the inmate had run out of the office into the unit. The operations lieutenant asked who the inmate was that had committed the assault. I told him that I would get the inmate, he told me that just give him the name and he would have the inmate locked up.

The inmate was placed in special housing. In his cell he had his property already packed in a duffle bag. It was determined the inmate had done a protective custody move. My sliding glass door was replaced with a metal door and frame.

Chapter 9

COMPUTER SPECIALIST

One day during lunch while I was in the officer mess at the penitentiary when the warden came up to me while I was getting a signature from a unit manager. He stated in a really loud voice that he wanted the attention of all the staff members present. He had an announcement to make. He told everyone present he wanted to introduce the newest computer specialist for the penitentiary. He shook my hand and told me congratulations on my selection. He had caught me off guard. He liked to do that to staff members in announcing promotions and transfers. He told me to report to personnel for a new name tag.

Later I asked when my reporting date was to the computer services department. I was now promoted to the grade of GS-11. I had spent just about 11 years at the penitentiary and had been promoted to the mid-level grade without having to move anywhere.

I was becoming a homesteader. I figured I would retire at this grade. I did not want to become a unit manager. The associate warden for custody did not want to release me right away to work in computer services. It finally came down to the warden ordering that I begin the computer job at the start of the very next pay period.

The name tag for a computer specialist is an ordinary blue staff name tag. Computer services was a new department and only had my boss the Computer Services Manager (CSM) and his assistant, me. The office was located on the second floor of the penitentiary hospital in an open bay used as a storage area.

Our server room was located in a secure area next to the lock shop and had a cipher lock on the door. The keys were restricted and under glass. We shared the telephone room and the telephone lines in the tunnel of the prison with the communications department.

One thing about being a computer specialist, we had access to anywhere in the prison, could be issued just about any key set, and had no real restrictions where we could go. We had access to any computer, any computer file and any authorized program. We could draw any tool from the tool room and our issue keys got us to just about any location within the prison. We had no time restrictions for work and generally worked a day shift with week ends and holiday's off. We were subject to being called into work at anytime there was a computer problem.

To me this was the best, but hardest jobs ever in the prison. You had multi task, set priorities, and get the job done. The pressure was always there. There were very few down times that you could just sit back and relax.

The boss was a communications expert, electronics expert, a computer expert, and a highly qualified bench technician. He was not that good performing administrative work. Administrative tasks were not his main interest in life. He did like being the duty officer.

When I first started in the department our mandate was to install a complete network including cabling, internal wiring, work stations, software, and provide for staff training. We were to install the network servers and make sure the system worked.

WALKING MAINLINE

Our first load of 226 computers all had to be brought into the prison, screened for contraband, software installed by hand, issued to staff, hooked up, and training on how to use the computers had to be given. This was not an easy job for two people to accomplish in a building that was built in the 1940's.

We had a contractor crew that we used to install the cabling, conduit, and all the hardware. The problem was they never did this type of work before. The crew had experience installing pools and spa's, not the electronic backbone for a computer system. We were restricted in obtaining the services of the local computer network system experts.

The first year the hours were really long and tiring. My boss worked with the contractors under the units, in the tunnel, and all over the prison drilling holes, putting in conduit, pulling cable, and termination of the cable ends to hook up the computers.

My job was to bring in the computers, monitors, keyboards, and everything else, install the software and get each work station ready. I also became an expert of installing the connectors for the computer work stations.

It seemed like years before we finally had two more staff added to the department. The one guy in our department was carefully trained by the boss in computer hardware. I became an expert in the administration of the system. We were always short handed.

We provided the mandated training to staff and had a very good computer lab set up for this training. I became a primary trainer for new staff and during our annual refresher training class.

WALKING MAINLINE

Beside all the work we also had to conduct computer related investigations of staff and inmates. The results of the investigations could lead to criminal prosecution and the firing of staff.

I also continued my NCIC certification so contractors and other cleared personnel could be escorted into the prison to perform work on the system.

The best thing about our location on the second floor of the hospital was that we had an elevator that we was used to bring in the computers and other equipment that we needed. We did not have to carry all the computer equipment up and down a stairway.

Being on the inside of the institution did bring up some security concerns about the introduction of contraband. We did not allow inmates to handle any of the staff computer equipment. All delivery of the computers would arrive at our outside warehouse and would be secured in what was called the hot cages. These were the locked storage areas inside the ware house. For a time if the computer or equipment box was still factory sealed, it was brought in through the rear sally port and taken for break down and storage in our office.

Soon it got to be a problem for storage of the boxes and packing. The procedure was changed on how the computers were unpacked, examined, and stored in the hot cages before being brought into the prison. When the department moved to the second floor location above the control room there was more storage room. A really large area was set aside for the old used equipment. It was a lot of work to clear the computers and get them ready to be disposed of. Some of the computers were donated to the local school system.

The original cabling for the system was for token ring. Token ring outlived its usefulness and an upgrade to ethernet was made. The system increase in speed was made by the adding of fiber optic cables and new hardware to handle the computer traffic. It does not matter how much you improve the system the end user will still complain the system is too slow or too complicated to use. It is truly amazing how much impact computers have had for correctional work. Of all the tools and equipment performing the job still comes down to working with inmates.

One of the jobs of computer services was to create and monitor the inmate access to the inmate computers. There was a problem with staff allowing inmate's access to staff computers and to information that was not allowed to be seen by inmates. In order for an inmate to have computer access a request had to be made by a staff member. The central file, sentencing files, and other information would be checked and the inmate would be placed on a computer "YES" list. Computer "NO" listing meant the inmate would not be allowed on an inmate computer. Certain computers for education classes were allowed. Regular inspections and review of inmate computers were conducted to insure compliance with policy and the law. Conviction of a computer crime was a computer "NO" for the inmate.

A few times staff would allow inmates access to sensitive information, and the excuse may be that, "Well the inmate was just helping," or some other reason. This could get a staff member fired or convicted of a criminal act.

WALKING MAINLINE

Even though we instructed staff about having pornographic files on computers, or bringing computer games from home and using work computers for games and other unauthorized use. Staff would still do bad things with computers. In the BOP a few staff members were convicted of computer crimes. The computer services staff would try to prevent staff from doing wrong but it would be done. Then there is no choice but to prosecute.

My last day of working in the department was filled with a lot of work, as I was out-processing I was thinking of all the projects that needed to get done. When I was going home for the last time my comment and thought was for my co-worker, "It was his entire problem now."

When an institutional emergency event happened, all staff responded. We are all correctional workers first. Many a time I responded to a call for assistance. Most of the time, I would hope for a false alarm.

One time while my boss and my co-worker were standing in line in front of control to turn in our keys, I saw an inmate on inmate assault taking place in front of "F" unit. I responded from the line at the same time the unit officers were calling for assistance. I saw an inmate with a weapon in his hand cutting the face and upper body of another inmate.

The two unit officers were taking down one of the inmates, I grabbed the inmate with the weapon in his hand and took him to the floor. I had the inmate by the wrist in a restraint hold he could not get out of. The problem was I could not cuff him. I called for hand cuffs while I held the inmate down. I told him that I had his knife. I was lucky and he stopped his struggle. One of the responding officers helped hand cuff the inmate and we escorted him to the lieutenant's office while other staff took the victim to the hospital.

Just after I released the inmate in the lieutenart's office I found an unused computer, wrote my supporting memorandum of what I had done during the response and was on the way home in less than 20 minutes time. I let the officers write the incident reports charging the inmates with fighting, assault, and conveyance of a weapon. It was the end of a routine day.

As a computer specialist I was out and about the prison as much as any staff member. I could be almost anywhere at any time.

During my last year, my assignment was to review the prison across from the penitentiary, the Federal Correctional Institution (FCI). It was a very different place from a penitentiary. The computer system was set up with individual profiles. Each computer would have extra profiles on the hard drive taking up so much space that it would block and slow down the operation of the computer.

The computer system that was in place at the FCI was far different from what was called for under the bureau guidance. It was not the same setup as at the penitentiary. It was very hard to reconcile the operation to what the bureau standards were. It took a long time, a lot of hard work, and money upgrading the computer system for the whole complex.

During the time I was assigned to the FCI the bureau decided to have all laptop computers turned in. Staff were not allowed the issue of laptop computer systems and could no longer take the systems to their homes to work on them. We had stacks of laptop computers in our storage area.

It took a very long time to set up the inmate computer "YES" and computer "NO" listings. The number of inmates that were serving time for computer crime was way more than at the penitentiary. The process took a lot of effort for the review of the inmate central files.

One problem that would shut down the fiber optic systems were mice. Mice liked to chew the fiber cables and cut them in half. Once the cable was damaged, we would have outside contractors either splice new cable or re-terminate the connectors to get the system back to operational status.

We had one time a broken wire that shut down the whole computer system communication's to the outside world. The telephone company employee and I had to hand check each circuit wire and finally after hours of work found one wire that was broken inside the insulation. Once that single wire was replaced the system was back on line. It was just incredible that one small wire would shut down hundreds of computers.

The way the prison complex was so dependant upon computers was just amazing. When I started in government service, we used typewriters and sheets of carbon paper. Copy machines were large and broke down many times during use. After a time the computers and network printers replaced typewriters and carbon paper. We were supposed to be more efficient and faster in our work. That is until the power went out.

When a power outage occurred, things were brought to a stand still. The cell doors were operated by electric motors.

WALKING MAINLINE

The lights would go out. The computer system would shut down and work would stop. The sally ports were run by electricity and the emergency gates would have to be operated manually. For the most part when the power went down it was not for a very long time.

After the power was restored was the time for hard work by computer services department. It sometimes took hours to restore the computer network to full operation.

Chapter 10

DEATH

Death was part of the job. I always hoped that whomever died in the penitentiary was not a staff member and we tried our best to insure the safety of staff and inmates. There is no particular order to the following events.

The saying at the penitentiary when I first started working there in 1985 was that until you experienced the first killing you were still a rookie. It was during the month of July 1985, the 4th month of working as a correctional officer my first response to a killing had taken place.

The event occurred during the day shift, a call for all radio units to respond to the 2nd floor of "I" unit was made by control. I responded as did a hundred other staff, it seemed like a hundred, maybe more like 50 or 60 staff. I helped carry the inmate victim from his cell on "C" range in upper "I" unit, past the range grill door, past the stairway grill door, down the stairway and out the food trap main door, where the inmate was placed on a hospital gurney and taken to the emergency room in the prison hospital. This all took less than five minutes.

As far as I could tell the inmate was dead. It was a standard procedure that an inmate would be rushed to the local hospital then pronounced dead on arrival or he would die at the local hospital. Inmates were not supposed to die in the prison.

I was returning to my post when another staff member asked me where I got the blood on my shirt. I looked and my sleeve of my shirt was bloody. I looked at my brand new blue blazer and the sleeve was soaked with blood, it was pretty messed up. I was allowed to go home and change my clothes and return to duty. I had to write my memo concerning my actions in responding to the killing. The memo had to be completed by the end of the shift and before I went home.

It was one of my classmates from the April Fools class that discovered the inmate had been stabbed. One of the inmates called the weapon used a "Snap on Shank." In reality it was a round rod sharpened to a point with a cloth handle. The inmate who stabbed the victim had pushed the rod between the ribs of the inmate just under the arm pit area. The rod penetrated the lungs and heart. The hole was very small and the victim inmate bled to death. He was lying in the upper bunk bed locked in the cell of a locked down special housing unit. I don't recall the reason why the inmate was killed.

I used to keep a listing of inmates killed during the time I worked at the penitentiary, and it was a really long list.

I was working an overtime shift in three tower. This is a pretty quiet tower in the corner of the institution overlooking the prison industries complex. We heard a call for assistance in "M" Mary unit. Listening to the control room officer on the tower intercom system respond to the radio traffic, make the phone calls for an ambulance and other activity. It was clear that a killing had taken place and a staff member might have been involved.

We heard an assault had taken place on "A" range. I had mentioned a certain inmate's name who could have been the victim. After other tower officers made phone calls to the unit officer, the story was that an inmate, the one I mentioned was standing outside a cell on "A" range of the holdover unit and was just looking into the cell. Apparently the two inmates assigned to the cell were doing drugs or something like that. One of the inmates got a hold of a prison made knife and proceeded to assault the inmate looking into the cell, while an officer was making his rounds of the unit.

The officer grabbed a garbage can lid and was using it as a shield against the inmate with the knife. The officer had activated his body alarm and staff responded to the call for assistance. The inmate who was looking into the cell had been stabbed several times and was bleeding to death. The inmate died on the way to the hospital.

Later during the shift I was told I had nailed it when I mentioned the name of the inmate. It was that inmate who was killed. I had worked the unit earlier and the inmate that was killed was on very heavy medication. He was in a type of stupor from the medication and it made him look like he was watching or just looking off into space. The medicine was prescribed for a seizure condition.

When I first became a counselor in "J" unit the evening watch officer and I were working on cell searches. He was a pretty good officer. He was killed in an off duty motorcycle accident just west on Lompoc on state highway 246. He was riding into town with a woman riding on the back of his motorcycle when he ran off the road.

I had training as an army accident investigator and looked into the accident. I was concerned that the conclusions made at the accident site were in error. I noted that when the motorcycle left the road it struck the edge of a concrete culvert causing front wheel damage, and flipping the motorcycle into a barbed wire fence.

I heard about the accident and went to the scene a day after it happened. I was taking photographs of the road and the path of the motorcycle. I saw tire scuff marks on the edge of the culvert and took photographs of that spot. I saw the motorcycle in the impound yard, looked at the damage to the front wheel, and took photographs of it.

It appeared to me that the officer tried to avoid a vehicle that crossed the center line and he took to the ditch. If it was not for the concrete corner of the culvert the motorcycle would have just slid along the grass in the ditch and the injuries would not have been fatal. I put together an information packet and forwarded it to the officer's father. The fact was that the officer was still dead from the accident.

We had an incident that took place while several correctional officers were off duty. They were drinking at the apartment of one of the officers. An officer who was a former member of the US Army had a .45 caliber pistol. He decided to show off the weapon during the party.

One of the officers had pulled back the slide of the pistol, let it go, and a round was loaded into the chamber. The officer pointed the weapon at another officer and pulled the trigger. The weapon discharged. That officer was hit in the chest by a 240-grain .45 caliber pistol round and died. It was a stupid mistake and accident. The officer who fired the weapon was convicted in court for the killing and sent to state prison.

I was working an evening watch shift as the control room officer. The "C" unit officer had called in his count to control, the shift lieutenant had taken the count and said it was a good count. Just about a minute later I get a telephone call on the inside phone from the same unit officer, he told me that he had a dead inmate in his unit.

This meant that he called in a count that was supposed to include living breathing inmates. I gave the telephone to the shift lieutenant who spoke with the officer for a minute or so. The lieutenant slammed down the telephone so hard that it shattered the telephone set. The lieutenant left control to go to the unit, while he was leaving the control room he told me to take the count, and make sure the staff were counting living breathing inmates.

Apparently the inmate was killed during the morning of the day shift. He was killed in the shower room, put on a wool army blanket, dragged to a cell and placed in the bunk. It was the wrong cell. The inmate whose cell it was assigned to, had the inmate put on a blanket, dragged across the floor in front of the officer's station, and the inmate was then put in his assigned cell.

The inmate was stiff from rigor mortis. The officer had counted the inmate and tried to revive the inmate. After he discovered that the inmate was dead and stiff, he had called in the count, then called me in control. I notified the county coroner and the institutional duty officer about the death. The inmate had to be removed from the prison by using the back fire escape door.

The officer received a reprimand for counting a dead inmate. He was also told that he should have walked around his unit during his shift so he could notice a dead inmate. You could see the drag marks on the floor where the inmate was pulled around on the army blanket.

WALKING MAINLINE

One day while I was arriving at the prison for work, I saw an ambulance leaving with lights and siren on. There was no chase vehicle. That meant only one thing; we had a staff member down. That ambulance leaving was a bad sign. I reported to the front of the institution and was told that a staff member was killed in "L" Lincoln unit. That was the unit I was assigned to as a counselor.

I bypassed the routine of reporting to the visiting room for assignment that was the normal procedure in an emergency situation. I picked up my keys from control and reported to my unit. When I arrived, the unit was being locked down. There was blood on the floor at the front door. There was blood on the stairway leading to the third tier, and there was blood on the floor of "F" range. It was a very bad sight to see all the blood.

I got to my unit team office where a briefing was taking place. As normal during emergency events sometimes the information given is wrong. The call for assistance was made by the unit officer, he had observed an inmate assaulted on "F" range, on third tier of the unit. The inmate had been stabbed several times in the back. The prison-made weapon was sticking out of the shoulder of the inmate, and he had died from the assault.

A staff member, who was a paint foreman in mechanical services had responded to the third tier where the inmate was assaulted. When the staff member got to the top of the stairs, he suffered a heart attack and fell to the floor. He was taken by staff to a waiting ambulance and was dead on arrival at the local hospital. He was a good friend, great co-worker, and drinking buddy. He died from the heart attack while on duty doing the job he loved.

WALKING MAINLINE

A few months later, while the case manager and I were getting ready to leave "L" unit for a Warden's recall the unit officer told us that he had a drunken inmate. I knew the inmate and he had a record of getting intoxicated on prison made "pruno," a drink containing alcohol. The inmate was escorted to the lieutenant's office. We went to our training center to listen to what the warden had to say. After a few minutes at the training center we were told that there was an inmate killing in "L" unit, the unit we just left. We asked how this event can happen in such a short time.

We returned to the unit, after drawing my keys from control I went to our prison hospital and spoke with the doctor on duty. He told me originally the inmate was brought to the hospital to be evaluated for being drunk. The doctor said the physician's assistant was looking at the inmate when the inmate collapsed to the floor. The inmate was having red colored foam coming out of his mouth. The inmate was strip searched and it was discovered he had a small round wound just under his arm pit. There was a small amount of blood coming out of the hole. The inmate had been stabbed in his heart. He died of this small wound. There was a lot of internal bleeding.

While I was the Officer in Charge (O.I.C.) of the Federal Prison Camp just as we were starting the 4:00 P.M. count one of the cowboy crew staff supervisor's stopped to tell me of a horse accident that involved one of the inmates. The inmate and his brother were rounding up cattle for branding on the Air Force base where the BOP leased land for livestock operations, when the horse the inmate was riding stepped in a prairie dog hole and fell on top of him.

WALKING MAINLINE

The inmate was taken to a nearby hospital. During the examination in the emergency room the doctors determined that the inmate had suffered a broken neck and other injuries. The inmate was placed in the intensive care unit. I had notified the inmate's unit team, and the inmate was placed on furlough status to the local hospital.

It was later determined by the doctors that the inmate was brain dead and the family was notified. The inmate was kept on life support for a few days while the family members were allowed to visit.

It was during the first part of an evening shift while I was the officer in charge at the prison camp, I received a telephone call from the doctor at the hospital. The doctor told me that the family had consented to taking the inmate off life support. I asked the doctor to notify us when the inmate died.

About a half hour later I received a call from the doctor who said the inmate had been pronounced dead. I told the doctor to hold for a minute and I contacted the camp lieutenant and informed him that he had a telephone call. He took the call and told me "Thanks a lot," now he had more work to do.

I had informed the doctor we would have staff come to the hospital to take finger prints and provide a positive identification of the inmate before he could be released to the funeral home. Normally when an inmate death occurs while they are on an escorted trip or furlough we would have staff take finger prints, make a positive identification, notify the next of kin, and perform all the administrative paperwork required. In this case the family was already notified.

WALKING MAINLINE

It was Monday, August 9, 1989 and I was working on the shakedown crew at about 8:00 A.M.. We were working on our search schedule for the day. I heard a radio call from control for the hospital doctor to report to the third tier of "F" unit. I told my partner that we had a body in "F" unit and we were going to there to provide assistance.

He looked at me and I told him that I had worked control for a long time and never called for a doctor to report to a unit. We went to the unit and arrived to a cell on the third tier where the doctor had just entered. There was an inmate lying on the bunk. The doctor grabbed the inmate by his elbow and rocked him back and forth. The inmate was stiff.

The doctor said the inmate was dead and probably died during the night before. The assigned FBI agent arrived and went into the cell. He grabbed the inmate by the elbow, rocked him back and forth and said "I can confirm that he is dead." By that time I was getting a tremendous migraine head ache. The investigative lieutenant arrived and looked in the cell and said "Yep the inmate is dead." The FBI agent requested that the shakedown crew look for a weapon outside the unit.

We went outside the cell block to conduct an extensive search of the ground. We were standing back some distance from the unit and were waiting. Inmates were tossing contraband out the windows while staff were conducting cell searches. When searching the ground outside the cell block I had found and marked what I thought could be a weapon used in the murder. Other staff helping in the search kept telling me no way what I found was the weapon.

WALKING MAINLINE

The FBI Agent looked at what I had found and said it looked like the weapon used and asked me to collect it, tag it with an evidence tag, and turn it in. I also had to write my memo about the incident.

The prison news release stated that an inmate had been murdered in a prison cell. It was one of the few times a statement of that kind was released. I was not required to testify in the court trial. It was determined that the inmate had been killed during the late evening shift before the inmates were locked down for the night.

During the morning watch shift counts, even though the inmate was dead and stiff, he was counted by staff. The inmate was discovered by the unit counselor during the morning census count. The BOP policy is to count living, breathing, inmates. In this case it was not done.

It was reported by news media on September 7, 1994, that an inmate was convicted of strangling a fellow inmate to get into a prison gang. A federal jury found that the inmate used a garrote made of bed sheets to kill another inmate as he lay on his cell bunk bed in a heroin-induced stupor. The killing took place at the Lompoc federal penitentiary on August 9, 1989.

It was on a Monday, December 28, 1992, while I was workings as a correctional counselor for "J" unit. The control room officer made the all radio units call for assistance. The call was for one of the inmates on my case load. He was a victim of a beating by another inmate who used a metal bar to assault him. The inmate victim later died.

The inmate killed was an inmate that I had refused to move into my unit because I had concerns over his safety. The associate warden over custody had ordered me to move the inmate from another unit into my housing unit. I wrote a protest memo for the record. During the FBI investigation of the killing that memo became an important piece of evidence.

February 8, 1993, it was a Monday at about 9:10 A.M.. Movement to the yard was delayed from the 7:40 A.M. work call to just after 9:00 A.M. because of light rain. I was a correctional counselor working as the unit officer for "J" Joker unit. It was during annual refresher training relief. I had joked with the unit manager the week before that I could not work a unit more than an hour when an inmate assault or killing would occur.

I had just opened the unit's front door for an activity and yard movement when I was informed by an inmate going out the door that I had a man down on the flats. I looked down the flats and saw what appeared to be a pile of clothes on the floor about half way down "B" range. I took a few steps toward the scene and saw it was an inmate down and bleeding. I activated my body alarm after I had muttered the words "Aw Shit!" and locked the front entrance door.

I started to run to where the inmate was down, and he was bleeding from stab wounds to his shoulders and chest. I stood just beside his cell door pushing back the curtain to insure I did not trap an inmate in the cell. I did not want to have to fight an inmate with a knife. It seemed like forever before the first staff member came through the door responding to the emergency.

My radio battery had died and I could not tell control what was going on. I could swear that responding staff had stopped for a barbecue and beer before they came through the door. When staff are responding to a call for assistance you first hear the prison keys rattling, then what sounds like a herd of elephants running, it is a thundering sound. It is a sound that you do not forget.

I grabbed the first officer and told him to tell control, "J" Joker unit inmate down and bleeding," this would tell the hospital staff and control that the call for assistance was real and what type of response the hospital needed to do.

The inmate was removed from the unit, and I went into my unit team office where the unit manager was working. I told him we just had an inmate assault in the unit. He looked at me and just said "What?" I was relieved from my post so I could write my memo for the investigators. I went to the second floor administrative building to the unit team office to look up the inmate's central file.

As I was writing my memo, I was being called by the special investigative supervisor's technician to find out where I was. I called the office and told them that I was writing the memo. Then I was called by the FBI for an interview. I finished my memo. I would like to say it was well written and described the scene and events of the killing. I also drew a diagram of the scene using a stick man figure indicating the location of the inmate as I found him. The inmate was taken to the local hospital where he died.

It would seem this was an open and shut case. I was called to testify in this capital murder case. I reported for a conference with the United States Attorney's office and was joking with the attorney who was going to take the case to trial. I said we had lost evidence, we had no knife, and no other evidence other than some photographs. The attorney looked at me and asked "How did you know?" I was then told that much of the evidence was lost including the DNA evidence. The weapon was also lost.

I was also told that I was the primary witness in the case. I was to set the prison scene and describe the events as I saw them. Before I was able to testify I was sequestered for a few days. I read Tom Clancy novels while waiting. When I finally reached the witness stand, it seemed like a long time of being on the stand. I was thinking a day and a half, and I had to wait until the trial was over before I was released from court as a witness. The end result we went to trail a second time because of a problem with the jury on the first trial.

It was later that the inmates pled guilty in the case and were sentenced to more prison time.

It was late on a Thursday afternoon about 5:20 P.M. on April 3, 1997 when I left the computer services department office located on the second floor of the prison hospital. The count had cleared. I worked some extra time on getting computer work stations set up for installation in the prison. I walked down the main corridor past the large dining room. I said hello to the officers working the exit door and conducting searches of the inmates. It was a normal routine evening shift. I had worked this shift before doing the same searches of the inmates leaving the dining room many times when I was in custody. I went home.

I just arrived at my house when I received a telephone call that there was an institutional emergency and I was to return to the prison right away. When I drove back to the prison staff were arriving in large numbers and filling up the parking lot. I was told that more than one correctional officer and been assaulted and maybe killed. I reported to the visiting room.

WALKING MAINLINE

On the way to the visiting room I saw the plate glass door was broken and partly off its hinges. There was a blood trail in the middle of the floor. Inside the visiting room it was staff milling around and assignments being given out.

I was told to go to the main corridor and help escort inmates back to the cell blocks. I went to the auditorium to escort inmates back to their assigned units. One inmate that I had cuffed and was escorting dropped his eye glasses. I was not going to pick them up, the lieutenant told me it was okay to retrieve them and return them to the inmate. When I had cuffed and searched the inmate I was escorting he was shaking and told me they were not responsible for killing the officer.

We were escorting some of the inmates out and around the outside of the prison to their units to bypass where the assault on the officers took place. After escorting the inmate to his unit I returned by using the main corridor. I had to walk between the pools of blood on the floor. FBI agents were making sure that we did not disturb the crime scene.

Later during that evening control announced over the public address system that it was a closed corridor for staff. The inmates were locked down. This was the only time that the corridor was off limits for staff.

The FBI was reenacting the assault and wanted to insure staff was not in the way of the video taping. The inmate, who committed the assault, had killed one officer, and injuring at least three other officers, it all happened at 5:52 P.M.. The main corridor officer was killed.

WALKING MAINLINE

I along with a couple of other staff members watched the video tape that recorded the assault. The officer who was killed, even after he had been stabbed, was trying to come to the aid of the other injured officers.

The killing of the correctional officer is a life changing event. The names of the staff who were working at the penitentiary are on a large plaque at the front entrance to the prison. I wore a black mourning name tag until the day I retired in memorial of that officers service. I used the phrase "There are 28,800 seconds in an 8 hour shift, he made every one of his seconds count." He worked at the penitentiary for only four years.

The officer's funeral and memorial service was attended by thousands of law enforcement officers, correctional officers, the Attorney General of the United States and his co-workers at the penitentiary. It was a day that the warden allowed us to wind down and to remember the fallen officer.

It was during this time our transportation officer died. He had become sick and was admitted to the local hospital where he died. It was tragic that he died. His funeral was not as large as for the correctional officer but he did die working the job. The attendance of the services was by his close friends and family. I had worked with him during his time at the prison when he was a correctional officer before he was assigned to transportation.

Normally in a federal capital case, the trail is held within about a year and a half of the crime. The US Attorney determined the inmate who is suspected to have killed the officer would be prosecuted as a death penalty case. It has been years and the case has not been taken to trial.

CHAPTER 11

ASSAULTS

An assault can occur for almost any reason. Most of the time an assault does not result in death or serious injury. Assaults can be inmate on staff, inmate on inmate, staff on inmate, or staff on staff. Sometimes an assault can be committed by an outsider.

An assault is defined as a crime of violence against another person. An assault may refer to an act that causes another to fear an immediate harmful contact, whereas the actual contact itself is called "battery."

The United States Penitentiary Lompoc was one of the federal institutions with the highest rates of inmate assaults on staff.

Sometimes an inmate would just spit on a staff member. At times an inmate may mix up feces and urine and spray a staff member with this foul mixture. A few staff members would respond with violence to the inmate, and that action is against policy and the law. It may feel good but it is wrong.

I can only think of one instance where a staff member lost it and assaulted an inmate, it was done in front of other witnesses other than me. We all reported the incident and the staff member was reprimanded.

When I was a counselor making my rounds in a special housing unit one of the inmates on my case load got mad at me over some stamps he thought he was entitled to and spit in my face. I was making the rounds with the duty officer when this occurred. I left the tier, walked into the special housing lieutenant's office had a photo taken of me with the spit still on my face and shirt. I cleaned some of the spit off and had the hospital PA examine me, make the notes in my staff medical file, and I wrote the incident report on the inmate. I included a supporting memo describing the incident.

The inmate received the maximum administrative sanctions that could be given. I also wrote a memo to the warden requesting that I not have to have contact with the inmate and be relieved of my counselor duties towards this inmate. I was surprised and pleased that the warden approved the request and he informed me that I did not have to respond or have contact with the inmate.

The inmate received the minimum amount of administrative support from staff. The other inmates in the lock down unit heard about what he had done and told him he should never ever assault a counselor.

For several weeks the inmate used to call out my name when I was making rounds and said he was sorry about spitting in my face and he did not mean it. Within a few weeks he was transferred to another prison with the notation he was assaultive towards staff.

I was working the lock down unit as a rookie officer when an inmate reached out through the cell bars and grabbed my tie and shirt. I responded by grabbing the inmate by the wrist and by a combination of stepping back and falling downward slightly got the inmate to let go my tie and shirt. The inmate was pulled towards the cell bars when his face stopped him from coming through the cell.

I was wearing a clip-on tie and recovered the tie. I left the range and reported to the lieutenant about the incident. I also contacted the hospital PA so he could look at the injury to the inmate's face made by the bars. The lieutenant told me to write the inmate up for assault. The lieutenant being an old school correctional lieutenant told me that I should have brought him the arm of the inmate who had assaulted me.

It was my second year working at the prison when I was making rounds on the third tier of the hold over unit, I was just at the top of "E" range when I head a commotion on the flats. I looked over the rail and saw an inmate who was being escorted by the officer in charge and a lieutenant.

The inmate was fighting and hitting both staff members. I ran down the several flights of stairs and according to a staff witness who saw the event from the lock down unit door stated that I flew through the air and landed on top of the inmate. That stopped the inmate from assaulting the two staff members. I got the inmate hand cuffed and checked for injuries.

My memo concerning the incident read in part, "I observed the inmate assaulting the lieutenant and the officer in charge, I responded down the flights of stairs and placed my knee between the inmate's shoulders and he ceased to resist." The memo and the incident report were used as examples in training of how to write a descriptive reporting memorandum. My concern when I took the inmate down was breaking his arm or dislocating his shoulder. By the time the story was circulated around the inmates, it was said don't mess with Officer Todd, it was not worth it.

It was during an evening shift when a call for assistance came from the hobby shop. We responded and when I arrived with other staff we found an inmate bleeding from the back of his head. He had been hit with the claw end of a hammer. He was moving around in pain on the floor. We took him to our prison hospital for examination. It was a very serious injury. After looking at the damage to me it appeared fatal.

I was the officer in charge of escorting the inmate from the prison to the local hospital. At the local emergency room it was determined the inmate required care from a higher level trauma center about an hour away. The trip from Lompoc to the hospital was a fast one. It was very hard to keep up with the ambulance with the chase vehicle I was issued.

When we arrived at the hospital the security staff gave me an excellent briefing on how security arrangements would be made for this high security inmate. The attending neurologist said it was remarkable that the inmate had survived the attack. The claw hammer had crushed bone and cut muscle. The inmate underwent about an 18 hour surgery. He did recover.

A call for assistance in the gym during an early evening shift brought staff response to an inmate who had been stabbed in the head by a locker rod. A locker rod is about 18 inches long and ¼ inch in diameter. The rod was sticking out of the inmates head making it appear that he had a rabbit ear TV antenna growing. He was transported and treated at the local hospital.

We had an inmate who claimed he fell out of his top bunk and hit his head on the floor. It appeared that he had hit the floor several times. His face was crushed to the point it took over 20 hours of surgery to reconstruct. The surgeon removed part of the inmates rib to rebuild the cheek bone. I was an escorting officer on that medical trip. I had one of the other officers who could work a double shift to scrub up in order to provide coverage of the inmate in the operating room.

It was pretty amazing to see inmates survive some of the assaults. Many times the injuries appeared so bad that no one could survive, but the inmate would.

A few times an inmate would appear uninjured and yet died because of internal injuries.

The policy is to use only the necessary force needed to control the situation this included up and to the use of deadly force.

CHAPTER 12

SEX

According to the BOP inmate disciplinary policy sex is a prohibited act. Staff having sex with inmates is against the law. Depending on the circumstance's staff having sex with inmates can lead to conviction of a federal crime and up to a life sentence for the staff member.

Federal law makes it a criminal act to have sexual relations or sexual contact between prison staff and inmates according to 18 U.S.C. sections 2241, 2243, and 2244.

Staff cross the line when they have sex with an inmate. Once that compromise is made all kinds of things may happen. Pregnancy may occur, or the inmate may demand contraband be brought into the prison.

When staff are compromised, generally it is reported by inmates in about six months to a year. The inmates will use up the staff. Inmates will then trade this information concerning corrupt staff for a better time during confinement or some other favor.

Sex between inmates can happen. When staff observed a sex act, it is supposed to be reported, there is an incident report code for the act. Sometimes prison rape does occur.

While I was working an evening watch as a main corridor officer, we received a report the "F" unit officer thought he had a sexual assault in one of the cells. A newly committed inmate was assigned to his unit. The officer placed him to the next cell that the unit team had told him was open for assignment. The inmate appeared to have been assaulted.

I escorted the inmate to the hospital Physicians Assistant where he was examined. It was determined that he had been assaulted. The inmate was placed in administrative detention. The inmate's cell mate was taken for a strip search, the technical term is a visual search of the inmate's body. It appeared that he had cuts and bruising to his body. During the interview of the inmate he admitted to sexually assaulting his cell mate.

The only other time that I had a case of prison rape was when I was working the holdover unit. We had just received inmates from our receiving and discharge department. We housed a new inmate holdover in a cell on "B" range just before the evening count.

During the count I heard a cell door banging on "B" range of the unit. We responded to the cell where the noise was coming from and we saw an inmate being pushed against the cell door. The inmate behind him was committing a sex act on the victim. It was against his consent. It was a nice way of saying rape.

Medical treatment was provided to the victim and the inmate who assaulted him was placed in our detention unit. That was about the only other time I had run across a possible prison rape case.

There were many times that we would receive information on who was doing who. There would be inmates who controlled other inmates for favors that were taking place. Our job was to catch the inmates and the inmates job was to get away with it. The inmates have 24 hours a day, seven days a week to get away with everything they can.

WALKING MAINLINE

Our most famous case with sex between staff and inmates was a female correctional officer and an inmate in the penitentiary. It could be called the "Love Shack" incident. About the time I became a correctional counselor in 1990 female correctional officers were allowed to work in the US Penitentiary. I had a female correctional officer assigned to my unit. She was the one that would become the subject of the "Love Shack."

We would hear stories about the sexual appetite of staff, both male and female. Many times staff would want to check out the story. The story that was being told by inmates to staff, was that a female correctional officer was having sex with inmates in the recreational yard storage building.

This was the building that staff used to issue sporting equipment to the inmates, such as softball bats, footballs, and so on. The back tower officers were told to watch the recreation yard for any unusual activity during yard times. It was reported that a line of inmates would form outside the recreational building when this certain female officer worked the yard. She would be inside the building. The line formed at other than equipment issue or turn in times.

There was a report that this officer had brought her mother into the prison to take a guided tour. A staff member with permission could bring in outside people to take a tour of the prison. Generally the times for the visit was during the day shift. What was different about the officer was that she had brought her mother into the prison for an escorted tour during the evening hours and into a housing unit to visit with an inmate.

WALKING MAINLINE

This raised some concerns from the unit officer and members of the unit team. Staff wrote memo's for the record documenting the visit and how it was so unusual. An investigation followed and the officer resigned. About a year or so later I heard the report that she was found dead along an interstate highway somewhere in Georgia or Alabama. After she left the prison she had worked as a stripper in night clubs in the Los Angeles area.

I was working as the officer in charge of our segregation unit, "I" unit. My number two officer approached me about having to go home and check on his wife. It was a weekend and things were pretty much under control.

I contacted the operations lieutenant and told him that my number two officer wanted to go home and check on his wife. I told the boss the officer may be concerned about his wife having an affair. The lieutenant asked me what I thought, and I told him he needed to know and I could let him be gone for an hour. He lived on the reservation and the post would be covered. With the permission of the lieutenant, I told the officer he had to be back within the hour.

Now looking back with 20/20 hindsight it might not have been the best idea in the world to let an officer go home and catch his wife having an affair. Things can happen, really bad things can happen. The officer returned in about half an hour. He was pretty upset. He had caught his wife in bed with a fellow officer having sex. He said he was not really surprised but he was still hurt. He finished his shift.

The lieutenant was told what happened when he made his shift rounds. My number two officer kept his assignment, the other officer was reassigned to a different duty post and shift. He was allowed an expedited transfer to another prison.

The visiting room could be called the passion pit for inmates. Authorized and approved outside visitors including wives, girl friends, and others would come to visit inmates at the penitentiary or the prison camp. A few times the inmates would try to have sex with a visitor without getting caught.

Attorney visits would take place in what is called an attorney client room. This area was off the main visiting room and was more isolated. We had reports that one of the female attorney's for a high profile inmate may have been having sexual relations with the inmate.

During one of the visits court ordered monitoring was in place. The inmate and his attorney were in the attorney client visiting area. The female attorney was giving oral sex to the inmate when the visit was terminated. During the disciplinary hearing for the inmate after being asked if he wanted to see the video tape evidence against him, he plead that he committed the prohibited act. His visiting was suspended. The attorney was banned from visiting federal prisons and a report was made to the bar association.

I was working at the federal prison camp as the officer in charge one weekend when I received a call in camp control. It was the visiting room officer who called and stated he had an inmate getting oral sex from a female visitor. I passed this information to the camp lieutenant who asked me if the officer could see skin. The visiting room officer then told me that not really but the inmate's penis was in the visitor's mouth and the inmate's hips were moving up and down.

WALKING MAINLINE

The lieutenant departed the office in a hurried manner. The inmate had his visit terminated. He was then examined, evidence collected, and the inmate was placed in detention. He lost his visits for at least a year and the visitor was banned from visiting federal prisons.

A few times female visitors had to be told to wear proper attire. No see through clothes, they were to wear a bra, panties, and told not to expose themselves. Children were present in the visiting area and to act accordingly. There were a few times that a female visitor would be turned away for not wearing enough clothes, a dress too short, no underwear, or clothing that had too much cleavage showing.

The rules had to be changed for the seating of visitors so that inmates would not have sex in the visiting room. The visiting area did not have windows or booths. We did have a children's play area that was glassed in. Staff would patrol the visiting room to make sure that no sitting on the lap occurred. Staff had to make sure during the photo session that an inmate could have that the visitor would not slide her dress up for a quick sex session.

Each security level institution has to adapt the rules and policy to fit their location.

At the federal prison camp normally sexual acts were not a problem in the visiting room. The problem came from what would be called "Tree line furloughs." The only barrier for inmates is a line drawn on the road or the tree line indicating the out of bounds area. A few inmates would contact their wives or girl friends to meet in a car off the road or in a field for some car sex.

Before some of the local farm buildings were torn down, inmates could meet with girl friends in those buildings, have sex and be back at the camp before they were missing from count. Just across the river from the new prison camp were a group of one and two bedroom houses used for farm workers. This would be where some of the meetings took place. They have been since been torn down.

A few times inmates may have been able to visit a local motel to have some sex.

We did have an incident out on the local prison camp grounds where a female staff member was caught in the act having sex with an inmate. She resigned and is no longer employed by the BOP.

At the Lompoc prison facility it was a rumor among the inmates that a staff psychologist was having sexual relations in the department where she worked. An investigation was conducted and the director of the Bureau of Prisons was informed of the incident. The staff psychologist is no longer employed by the BOP.

In the penitentiary's special housing unit a male correctional officer was recorded on the video tape system having a sex act performed by a male inmate on him. The officer is no longer employed by the bureau of prisons.

Of all the rumors and stories I have heard, I did not hear any of camp inmates having sex with staff or members of the family on reservation housing. I was not privy to the entire goings on where staff lived in the prison reservation housing.

Having sex and affairs between staff, staff spouses, family, friends, and so on, are ongoing events. We would hear that so and so and his/her wife/husband have "split the sheets," and are separated, or going to be divorced. If the staff member lived in reservation housing, and the spouse was leaving, all kinds of administrative actions had to be accomplished. It could turn into a real mess.

CHAPTER 13

ESCAPES

The mission of the Federal Bureau of Prisons is the safety, care, and accountability of inmates that are in the custody and care of the United States Attorney General. To that end the BOP provides housing and is accountable for the inmates under its care.

The BOP has a system of counts. They have prisons with different levels of security. Those levels may be an open Federal Prison Camp, Federal Correctional Institution with fences, Federal Penitentiary with fences and gun towers, administrative facilities, and the Administrative Maximum Penitentiary. Each prison has it's own unique design and setup.

A few years before I started working at the penitentiary at Lompoc California, I saw a CBS 60 minutes report that told about "Club Fed," where a couple of Watergate burglars of the president Nixon era were housed. The federal prison camp at Lompoc was called "Club Fed." One of the burglars, a former FBI agent was housed in a higher level facility.

A federal prison camp is an open facility. The boundaries may be marked with a painted line, road, or even a tree line. There are no fences, and camp inmates are generally not a flight risk. Inmates may be serving sentences from a weekend to several years.

There are a few inmates that cannot adjust to the open life of the camp. I had one inmate that refused to work and wanted to transfer to a higher level federal prison. He was helped with his wish. A couple of years later he worked his way to the penitentiary. He did work for me inside the penitentiary for a time.

I was off duty returning from an out of town trip when I saw the sign placed along the highway into Lompoc. The sign was worded "Escaped Federal Prisoner," and a warning do not pick up hitchhikers. I called from my apartment and spoke with the operations lieutenant telling him I saw the sign about an escaped inmate. He told me not to worry it was just a camper and a "Walk Away."

He told me if it was an inmate from the penitentiary I would see staff at the escape posts with weapons, and I would have been called in to work. I was to report for my normal shift.

I always figured that when an inmate escaped, the tracking teams would be out with blood hounds, search teams would be looking, and all the other kinds of stuff would happen. There would be helicopters flying overhead, people would be told lock their doors, and stay indoors. There would be road blocks, cops every where and a whole lot of law enforcement to help find the escaped prisoner.

It was just a camper. In reality when the inmate is recaptured, no matter how long it takes, they are still an escaped federal prisoner subject to prosecution, getting a longer sentence and being placed in a higher level prison.

The Lompoc prison had a couple of wide publicity escapes. One of the inmates, who was involved with an espionage case escaped from the prison in 1980 when it was a lower level institution. He was later found by the US Marshal's Service and returned to custody.

On October 22, 1983, six inmates, escaped from the United States Penitentiary at Lompoc, California by driving the prison garbage truck through the recreation yard fence. A short distance from the fence, the truck, hit by gunfire from the towers, went out of control. It ran into the raodside dragon's teeth. One inmate died in the truck and the others were caught.

The escape, known as the "Trash Truck Escape" occurred before I started working for the BOP. I did know several of the staff who were involved in stopping the escape. The official after action review and report of the escape was part of our emergency procedures training.

I used to escort this same truck when it was taken inside the prison for trash runs. I always had a concern about inmates attempting to use this truck in another escape attempt.

On Friday, April 22 ,1989, we had two inmates escape from the penitentiary by hiding inside boxes being taken out of the institution. The inmates were seen by staff while they were running through the UNICOR warehouse area outside the penitentiary fence at about 2:10 P.M..

One of the inmates was caught right away. The other inmate ran into heavy brush at the back of the penitentiary. A ground and aerial search by helicopter was started. After a day or so the local search was called off. The US Marshal's service continued the search for the other inmate.

On Sunday, January 6, 1991, a convicted kidnaper, who had escaped from prisons and jails nine times, was taken into custody after he escaped from the penitentiary. We had over 400 BOP staff on a 31 hour escape hunt through heavy fog and really dense underbrush.

On Friday, November 15, 1991, we received a report from the Los Angeles Police Department three of our inmates had escaped while out on writ. It was during the early morning hours on Thursday the inmates attacked their escorts with chains and handcuffs during a fuel stop just outside of Santa Barbara. They drove away with the private escorts locked up in the back of the escort van. The escorts were later released. One of the inmates was on my case load. They were later recaptured.

It was in 1993 while I was working "L" Lincoln unit on a day shift. Staff had a report that two inmates escaped from the penitentiary by crawling into a storm drain that leads to the riverbed near prison.

Staff responded to where the drain pipe emptied into the river. Tracks were seen in the sand leading towards the ocean. After following the tracks for a short way everyone was called back to conduct an inside search of the prison. For a day or so a search was conducted inside the prison.

Several staff had brought up their concerns that the two inmates had escaped by going out the drain pipe. It was later learned the two inmates had gotten through a locked grill in the storm drain, ran down the river bed, and had made it to the railroad tracks. They then traveled along the coast towards Santa Barbara, California. Eventually they got to Las Vegas, Nevada where they were recaptured.

On November 9, 1994, the U.S. Marshal's Service in Las Vegas provided a news release stating that the two inmates who had escaped the Lompoc Penitentiary in 1993, were such a danger that 11 deputies had been assigned to guard them when their trial began in the U.S. District Court.

The Marshal's Service wanted to keep them in restraints during trial in Las Vegas. The two inmates made threats of violence and the escape had prompted the marshals to declare the inmates "The highest level of threat" to the community.

I was working as the main corridor officer during an evening shift and I was just ending the activity movement when I had an inmate running down the west corridor toward the gym grill. Since the announcement was made by control to end the movement, it would not be too unusual for an inmate to hurry in order not to miss going to the yard. I told the inmate to walk, and he slowed to a fast walk. As he got to the exit door to the recreation yard, he started to run across the yard.

What I heard later was that he ran down the dirt track that was in the recreation yard, then across the grass zone, past the out of bounds signs. A tower officer had yelled on a bull horn for the inmate to stop and get away from the fence. The inmate started to climb the inside fence. The tower officer seeing the inmate was trying to climb the fence and escape, fired a couple of rounds from his rifle. The inmate was hit in the shoulder muscle just above the collar bone.

No matter what you see on TV a high power bullet through the shoulder will slow you down. The inmate was down between the fences. Responding staff had to run out to the fence, around the end of the fence line, enter the gate, and get to the inmate.

The armed patrol officer covered the inmate with his weapon while staff were responding. When staff brought the inmate back into the prison, the shoulder wound looked really ugly. The inmate was given medical treatment that involved a trip to the local hospital.

One of the stories that went around was that the inmate was trying to commit "suicide by cop." The inmates used to say it was suicide to try and hit the fence with all the gun towers. I later talked with the officer who had shot and hit the inmate. He had told me that he was trying to fire warning shots, and it was a surprise when the inmate was hit. It was a moving target after all.

Not so long after that event we had an inmate that got the nickname "Air Vernon," escape. During evening yard, the inmate decided he would run for the fence. He did, he ran toward the fence that formed the western barrier on the recreation yard. He scaled the first fence, then it was noticed by tower officers that an inmate was between the fences and control was notified.

What was significant about this event, the inmate was climbing the outside fence, succeeded in getting over the fence, ran across the outside perimeter road, across the open field into the tree line. The responding armed patrol officer managed to fire a round at the escaping inmate. The prison was locked down and it was determined that an inmate had escaped. His name and description was sent to the local police and Vandenberg Air Force Base. An escape hunt for the inmate was started. No other shots were fired during the escape.

During the after action review, the tower officer who saw the escape told investigators that he could not shoot an inmate. He was unemployed by the end of the investigation.

I talked with him later and he told me he just could not shoot another human being. I told him all he had to do was fire some rounds into the ground if he did not want to shoot the inmate. I told him as long as he fired his weapon no one would have questioned him, he could have missed. I told him that even the best rifle shots could miss being nervous and the adrenalin flowing. If he had only fired his weapon, he could have kept his job.

The inmate who escaped stayed on the air force base for a time. He had been assigned to the base when he was on active duty with the air force before his conviction and transfer to the penitentiary.

We were called out to report for duty and report to an assigned escape post. One of my co-workers who was assigned to his post was approached by the local police department patrol officer. Someone had called 911 and told the operator they saw a man with a gun standing along a road by a river bed.

The officer told the staff member to put down his weapon. The staff member was armed with an M-14 military style rifle. The report was the staff member told the officer that his weapon was bigger and the officer should put his weapon away. A radio call by the officer to his dispatcher confirmed that the staff member was on duty and was authorized the weapon. The staff member continued his duty assignment.

During one of our annual refresher training sessions a video tape was shown about a tower officer who said he thought he fired five shotgun rounds during a recreation yard assault at another penitentiary. The video clearly shows that the officer had pumped all the rounds from the shotgun, but did not fire the weapon. It is a good guess that this action was due to the adrenalin and excitement of the moment and the officer thought he fired the weapon.

When shots are fired on the recreation yard, the reaction is to hit the ground. Both inmates and staff will go down. That is just human nature. Inmates will stay down when they are not involved with the event. Staff will respond and the most important part on the actions of the staff that have the weapons is not to get too excited and fire rounds at staff. Any movement will attract the shooter and it takes good training to control weapon's fire.

The BOP has some really good training video tapes. A couple of the scenes on that tape show just how fast an inmate can escape from a facility. I watched some kids scale an iron bar fence that would really take effort to climb even with a ladder. They went over the fence in seconds to play on the other side of the fence. When staff are on duty, the job is to prevent an inmate from escaping. The staff have to be alert so attention must not wander.

With all the security procedures in place, the system still can be beat if staff do not do their job. There have been a few times an inmate could just walk out with a crowd of staff when no one challenges them for identification.

I had an inmate assigned to my unit that was older, late 60's and he told me the story of his escape history. Years before while being escorted by two police officers on an airline trip, he announced to the stewardess that he was hijacking the aircraft.

He pointed out the two officers told her they had guns. She was to tell the pilot to fly at tree top level just like in World War II. The stewardess after seeing that one of the men did have a gun on his belt notified the pilot that the plane was being hijacked. The inmate told me that when the plane landed, all three of them were placed in hand cuffs and removed from the plane.

The two officers were released because they had their badges and ID's and he was arrested. He was tried in court and sentenced to several years in prison. He said the officers were pretty embarrassed to have their prisoner hijack the aircraft when they were transferring him.

When he was in prison he was transferred to a federal prison camp, and I was thinking this was at Lompoc. He walked away and became an escaped federal fugitive. While on escape status, he had gotten married, fathered children, and worked at a regular job. After a time he was divorced, lost his job, and became homeless.

He was in San Diego when he said he tried to turn himself in at the BOP facility there. Staff told him that no record existed of his conviction or escape status. He insisted that he was an escaped prisoner and he was turning himself in.

At some of the prison facilities homeless people try to turn themselves in for free meals and a place to sleep. He was told to come back the next day and give the staff time to research the files. He returned and was told to come back in a few days. He said when he came back again the US Marshal's were waiting for him, they hand cuffed him and hauled him off to jail. They had found his records. He was convicted and sentenced to serve his time at the penitentiary in Lompoc.

I was working his unit when he told me this story. Inmates can tell some pretty good stories about themselves and most of the time there is not much truth in the story. I reviewed his central inmate file and found that his story was true.

After a while I was assigned to work the control room. He used to come to my control room window and asked if I would let him out, it was a standing joke, I would say no, it was not his time yet. After a few months he looked in very bad shape, he was losing weight and looked sick. One day he was being taken out on a stretcher for an emergency air flight to the medical facility in Rochester Minnesota. He looked so bad that I figured he would die on the airplane.

A few months later I was working control when there was a tapping on the window of my control room. Normally that tapping on the control room window is a very big NO! NO! It was the same inmate being returned to the penitentiary.

He looked in really good shape. He said that the Mayo clinic had really treated his heart condition well and he felt better than ever. A couple of months later he tapped on the control window again and said that we were letting him go. This time he had the proper paperwork. I told him don't come back and it was nothing personal. Later that day I was notified by our R&D staff that he was released, the sentence complete, no probation, no supervision.

CHAPTER 14

RIOTS

A prison riot is an act of concerted defiance or disorder by a group of prisoners against the prison administrators, prison staff, or other groups of prisoners in an attempt to force change or express a grievance.

A prison riot can start over almost anything. The most likely location for a prison riot is the mess hall. Just about any location in the prison a riot may occur.

The following two riots are quite important in prison history of riots:

The Attica Prison riot occurred at the Attica penitentiary in Attica, New York, in 1971. The riot was based in part of the inmates concerns and demands for better living conditions.

On September 9, 1971 around 1,000 of the penitentiary's 2,200 inmates rioted and seized control of the prison. They took 33 staff hostage. The riot was also partly in response to the death of a black radical activist inmate, who had been shot to death by correctional officers at California's San Quentin penitentiary. It also was about overcrowding and other conditions at the prison. After the riot started New York state began negotiating with the prisoners.

During the following four days of negotiations, authorities agreed to some of the prisoner's demands. The governor then ordered state police take back control of the prison. Law enforcement opened fire on the recreation yard. During the riot 39 people were killed, including 10 correctional officers and staff.

WALKING MAINLINE

The New Mexico Penitentiary Riot, took place on the 2nd and 3rd of February, 1980, in the state's maximum security prison, just a few miles south of Santa Fe. It was a violent prison riot. There were 33 inmates killed, and at least 200 inmates injured. The total number of officers taken hostage was 12. None of the officers were killed. Several of the officers were treated for injuries caused by beatings and rape.

At times things did go crazy at the penitentiary in Lompoc. One day I was working the control room on a day watch shift when the warden called to tell me he would be on frequency two of the radio system if I needed to get in contact with him.

It would have been a quiet November 1987 shift. My SENTRY terminal screen beeped a very long beep and a large message scrolled across the screen. It read in part that the director of the Bureau of Prisons had sent out an important message to the Warden. I had not seen a message like this before.

I contacted the warden by radio and he told me to open his SENTRY mail box. I told him that I did not have his password. He said he did not have it either, and to contact his secretary at home.

The message was to the warden informing him that he was to assemble and send his disturbance control teams to the Atlanta Penitentiary in Georgia because the Cubans had taken over the prison.

Later the federal prison in Oakdale, Louisiana was also taken over by Cubans. I started calling off duty correctional staff so they could get ready for the trip. I volunteered to work double shifts in control. Later after the riot had ended, we received a couple of hundred of the Cubans. A lock down unit was prepared. Staff worked 24/7 in order to get that unit ready.

On 20 November 1987, the United States announced the reactivation of its 1984 immigration accord with Cuba. The agreement was negotiated after the military action in Grenada the year before.

This agreement had the return to Cuba of 201 Mariel Cubans detained in U.S. prisons. When the Cubans were returned, 73 of them were immediately put in prison when they arrived in Havana, Cuba.

The program was suspended by Fidel Castro during May 1985, in response to anticommunist Radio Marti broadcasts which were aimed at Cuba.

Immigration relations were restarted in 1987. This was a sign to the 2,563 Cubans who were being held in prison and detention centers across the United States the deportations were going to happen.

The Cubans had several concerns, they felt forgotten and abandoned. With the deportation program starting, the Cubans being held at the Detention Center in Oakdale Louisiana and the Federal Penitentiary in Atlanta Georgia rioted.

The Cubans took hostages and set fires at both prisons. After almost two weeks of negotiation and other actions both Oakdale and Atlanta were returned to bureau control.

A group of Cubans were transferred to USP Lompoc and placed in special housing. Detention hearings were also started.

When a riot does occur, the prison administration has emergency plans to contain, control, and end a riot. On paper it looks so good. In reality, well I use the term "It is like a Chinese Fire Drill," or a real "Charlie Fox Trot," some times a confusing mess that somehow sorts itself out.

It is no fun to report to an emergency situation, suit up in riot gear, then sit for hours waiting to be put in action. Most of the time, it is just a relief that you sit around waiting to be called, but not having to be called, and then be told to go home.

A couple of times I responded to the call for assistance and found I was in the middle of a riot. In one instance the riot resulted in the prison being locked down for almost three weeks.

There was one time we responded to a radio call for assistance that was a fight in the gym. The fight started over a disputed inmate referee call during a basketball game. All evening staff responded and the inmates involved were hand cuffed and removed from the area. I walked through the gym area, there were about 300 inmates in the gym.

The inmates started to get restless and were milling around. I looked around for any other staff, and there were none. I was the only staff member present. I decided that I needed some type of control of the situation, so I yelled out the command "Count Time." I yelled this command a couple of times.

The inmates were used to having a count in the gym. They all went and sat down in the bleachers. I ordered them to sit by their unit assignments, starting with "B" all the way to the end of the unit designations, that ended with "L" unit.

That took a few minutes for them to be organized. It got pretty quiet, a little strange when it gets quiet in a prison, generally that means something is going to happen.

I took a clip board with an out-count sheet on it and started the routine of taking the count. I was hoping that someone would notice that the inmates were still in the gym and send some staff to cover the area. After what seemed hours, about a dozen staff returned to the gym.

They asked me what was going on when they saw the inmates all sitting on the bleachers. I told them it was count time. The inmates were escorted by their unit assignment from the gym. While they were being taken from the gym a video camera crew was set up to get the names and numbers of the inmates on tape.

I was told later that it was a neat trick that I used to control the inmates in what could have been an ugly situation. I figured that if a single officer could call count and control a housing unit of 200 inmates, it could work in this situation, and it did.

During the day of August 28, 1989 a fight involving inmates from the East and West coasts took place at the penitentiary. The fight took place in the recreation yard of the penitentiary. This involved 40 to 50 inmates. It lasted for a short time. Staff responded and the penitentiary was placed on lock-down for a few days.

On August 24, 1991 the Cuban inmates at the penitentiary were placed on restriction because of hostage taking by the Cubans at the Talladega, Alabama Federal Correctional Institution. The inmates in Lompoc were released from the restriction after hostage situation was resolved.

WALKING MAINLINE

I knew the warden at Talladega. I worked for him when he was in charge of the Federal Prison Camp at Lompoc. I liked him. He was fair and friendly. He listened to staff and inmate concerns. He made a good supervisor. We had several of Lompoc penitentiary staff go on TDY to the situation in Alabama.

In 1995, a fight that began in the penitentiary dining room almost led to a takeover of the prison. Our Special Operations Response Team (SORT) for the penitentiary was used in response to the situation. Members of the team entered through the roof and stopped the disturbance by using flash bang grenades, CS gas, and dogs.

During this situation we responded to the chow hall and escorted inmates back to their units. It was during all the confusion I did get locked in a cell with an inmate.

I was in a cell block when the SORT team used flash bang grenades. It was a lot of noise and the CS gas stung the eyes. One of the correctional counselors got hit in the head by a pool ball. He was knocked down.

It was on Sunday June 1, 2003, a riot erupted inside the penitentiary with several inmates and correctional officers being hurt. The prison was placed on lock down for several days. The fight started when staff checked a unit where the inmates were drinking prison made intoxicants. Eight officers and one inmate received medical treatment at local hospitals after the incident.

It was on October 15, 2003 three correctional officers were stabbed by an inmate wielding a homemade prison knife.

It was on December 27, 2003 a fight in the dining hall between members of the crips and bloods street gangs had taken place.

WALKING MAINLINE

It was January 6, 2004, when the local American Federation of Government Employees (AFGE) Union wrote a letter to a US Senator. The union raised concerns that top prison officials ignored warnings of threats of violence where officers were injured and working conditions were unsafe.

It was in late January and early February 2004, the penitentiary was locked down for about three weeks after an inmate riot.

During this time an internal investigation was started by the central office concerning the problems with the penitentiary.

In March 2004, a Deputy Director for the Bureau of Prisons became the acting warden for the penitentiary. It was reported that the warden was asked to leave the prison. He announced his retirement from the Bureau of Prisons effective May 2004. He had been at the prison about 3 years.

It was during his time at the prison that allegations were made the prison had become unsafe to work in, he was biased towards inmates, lax on inmate discipline, obstructed an investigation, and other charges.

It was in April 2004 the central office announced that a warden from the U.S. Penitentiary Lee, Virginia was going to be the new warden. His start date was May 30, 2004.

After the new warden took over it was quiet at the penitentiary. He was my last warden that I worked for before I retired.

Chapter 15

ANNUAL REFRESHER TRAINING

According to published reports, there were 743 employees at the federal correctional complex in Lompoc. Scheduling that number of employees for annual refresher training is a very large task. The training department staff is small in number and does a very good job.

During my first year of employment at the penitentiary I went to institutional familiarization class, GLYNCO training academy, and annual refresher training (A.R.T.). A.R.T. is a week long session that all staff attended unless there is a proper excuse not to attend. Portions of the training such as self defense required a doctor's certification if you could not perform the physical requirements of the training. If you were excused, you would observe the training.

For many staff this training can be a boring time. I generally sat in the front row of class, always tried for the first or second weekly session and took lots of notes. The note taking kept me awake and busy. Much of the training was actually interesting and relevant to our jobs. The classes were taught by subject matter experts. For ten years I was one of the subject matter experts and instructor for the computer services training.

Each year the Bureau of Prisons would send out what would be mandated training, with lesson plans and instructional material for the training. Staff who were selected to be instructors had to complete instructor training for the courses.

137

WALKING MAINLINE

The training was held in our staff training center, away from the prison, and we would be allowed to wear regular street clothes for the classes.

A couple of times I attended A.R.T. with the warden and executive staff. It was a very good time to ask them questions that you would not otherwise dare to.

Our security officer, also known as the locksmith put on a very good slide show of events and happenings around the prison for the prior year. We had plenty of hands on training for prisoner escort, disturbance control, self defense, and other subjects.

Stomp and drag was one of the classes that staff would groan over. The real name of this class was disturbance control. In class we would suit up in riot gear. We would learn how to use the riot baton. A riot baton is a plastic like stick, just about three feet long with embedded round steel balls at each end placed there by the manufacturer. That is the description provided to us for training and use of force purposes. We would practice, strikes, parries, jabs, and other moves used to control inmates during a riot situation.

The stomp and drag was the way we moved in formation. If you see a formation of officers, dressed in helmets, pads, and all the riot gear, it is very impressive when a formation is in a controlled movement. It sends a very strong message. The stomping of the foot is a time or cadence marker while dragging the other foot was to maintain balance.

Several of the staff members had received extensive hand to hand and bayonet training in the military and could really put up a fight that would be hard to defeat.

A few of the films of riot control before I started working at the prison showed staff with pick axe handles and not much else for protection. Someone coming at you with a pick axe handle can be a very frightening sight.

Self defense classes at times had to be controlled so staff would not injure each other. Each staff member paired off with a partner to practice the move listed for training. Pay back was fair play, so care would be taken not to hurt anyone.

The first year of A.R.T. we practiced forced cell moves in a formal way. We had a lieutenant tell us to hit him at full speed. During that exercise six staff with a combined weight of 1200 to 1500 pounds hit the lieutenant. He was injured and after that no full speed forced cell move practice sessions during A.R.T. were done.

Talking about policy, and how we were to apply it, was pretty dry training. It took very creative instructors to keep the class awake and interested in the classes. The use of small candy bars was an effective tool to keep a class alert. Some departments had the class play games designed around the annual refresher training subjects.

Firearms' training was the part of the A.R.T. class that I liked the best. We were firing for qualification with the handgun, rifle, and shotgun.

For a most of my career we fired the M-14 rifle, a .308 caliber weapon that could reach out 1,000 yards and take down a person. The weapon weights 10 to 12 pounds and does have some recoil.

The 12 gauge shotgun, loaded with double 00 buckshot is a weapon that street criminals know well and show a lot of respect for. If you do not hold the shotgun properly, you can get some pretty bad bruises from firing the weapon.

WALKING MAINLINE

For the handguns we had revolvers that only five rounds were loaded into. It was later during my career the transition to a semiautomatic 9mm pistol was made. When we first began qualification with this weapon, I was able to fire hundreds of rounds. I was on the range for a whole day of training. To me this was a really good time.

All staff with a couple of exceptions had to qualify yearly with all three weapons. Range safety was very important and the instructors were the best.

All in all annual refresher training is an important element of working in the prison environment.

WALKING MAINLINE

Chapter 16

Admission and Orientation (A&O)

Admission and Orientation is a program that all inmates have to attend. This is the program where inmates are told what is expected of them, their rights and responsibilities, and how they are to be treated by staff. Each inmate that is processed into the prison is provided an A&O hand book. They sign for the book and the form is filed in the inmates central file.

The A&O handbook contains information about the prison, how quarters assignments are made, how work assignments are made, the rules and regulations that apply to the inmate.

The institutional familiarization class for staff would equate to the A&O program for inmates.

I was assigned as the A&O/UNICOR correctional counselor. One of the jobs of the A&O counselor is to review the US Marshal's list of inmates designated for the prison. From that list unit team assignments were made. Classes had to be arranged for inmates who would be placed in general population. The work assignment of A&O was made. All initial work assignments from the A&O program were made by the A&O counselor.

A callout sheet, which is a listing of where and when inmates were supposed to report for A&O and other assignments, would be published for each work day. The A&O class was a mandatory assignment for inmates. If an inmate refused to report for his A&O class, he would receive an incident report and be placed in detention. The incident report would be written for refusing a work assignment, refusing programs, and depending where the inmate was during the time of the A&O class he could be charged with other offenses, such as being in an unauthorized area.

During the time I was the A&O counselor I did not have problems with inmates being a no show. I was assigned as the A&O counselor for over two years.

When I conducted the A&O class I would greet the inmates with my standard, Welcome to U.S.P. Lompoc speech. I would tell the inmates "Welcome to U.S.P. Lompoc, where we don't care and you can't make us. You ain't got nothing coming. Let me tell you how it is to do time here. Don't gamble, pay your debts, don't do drugs, don't take it up the butt, and do your own time."

There was a shock value to my statement. It got the attention of the inmates. The old timer's knew what I was talking about. I did not sugar coat anything and gave it straight to the inmates. I would explain what was expected of the inmates and tell them how the A&O class would proceed.

Each department head was responsible for his section of A&O and was scheduled to give their portion of the class. We met the program and policy statements. Since I was also the UNICOR counselor. I would insure that the inmates who wanted a UNICOR job had filled out an application for placement on the UNICOR waiting list.

Every inmate that went through the A&O program required documentation. Those forms were filed in the inmate's central file. The A&O counselor kept a copy for his records. This was an item that a program review team would look for during their inspection visit.

An A&O counselor desk book was created that also was the S.O.P. for the program. One of the requirements of the A&O/UNICOR counselor was to make weekly rounds of the work and recreational areas of the inmates. The prison industry factories were visited three times a week to take care of the administrative needs of the inmates. There was an office for the counselor out in the cable factory of the prison. This was where inmates could have approved telephone calls to the courts or their attorney for current court cases.

The assignment as an A&O/UNICOR counselor was a very busy one that made the time go pretty fast. This was my last assignment before I was selected as a computer specialist. The assignment to this position was rotated generally every two to three years.

The boss for the position was the case management coordinator. Day to day supervision was not needed for the counselor. The paperwork was a very large amount and could be quickly taken care of.

Chapter 17

BORED

If you got bored working at the prison, then there was one very important rule, don't fall asleep. Sleeping on the job is a very big NO! NO! Many times working a morning watch tower or armed patrol it was so hard to stay awake. Just standing up and walking around would help. Even working a morning watch in a unit would often be boring. During long hours of hospital duty staff could get sleepy.

There was one simple rule, you sleep on the job, you could die! I did not want to die! During a lot of shifts it would be boring. Reading policy sounds very boring, but writing out suggestions on changing local policy, and submitting them would keep you busy during a shift. Many times the suggestions would be accepted and put in local policy.

When working a unit to keep from getting bored, take a walk though the unit on each of the tiers, and talk with the inmates. Perform cell searches. Learn the unit or the work site.

Quite a bit of the time working a post is just standing there and watching an open door, hallway, or even a waiting line of inmates while nothing really happens.

Working morning watch gun towers would get really boring and tiresome at about 2:30 A.M.. I used to tell my fellow tower officers to take a sharpened pencil, hold the pointed end up on the desk in front of you, if you nodded off your head would hit the pencil point and that would wake you up. Doing that could hurt.

WALKING MAINLINE

Cleaning and making things look good and orderly is a never-ending job. This can be done to keep from getting bored.

During the slow times in control it was a good idea to learn and review all the SENTRY commands. It was also a great idea to know the emergency plans in detail.

A few staff with computer access would bring in their own computer game programs. This was not allowed by policy and could get the staff member into a lot of trouble, maybe even fired.

For the most part a boring shift is good. Nothing out of the ordinary takes place and you can go home at the end of shift. That is a good deal.

Chapter 18

COMPUTERS

SENTRY is a data management system used in the Federal Bureau of Prisons for inmate information.

When I started in 1985 there were very few computers in the prison. The inmate data system named SENTRY was just being installed. This system had terminals installed in control, one terminal for the east end housing units, one terminal for the west end housing units, a terminal in receiving and discharge, one terminal at camp control, one for camp receiving and discharge, a case management coordinator terminal, and an inmate system manager terminal.

The terminal operator had to learn various commands in order to obtain information about inmates from the system. The terminal had a GO! Prompt. If you did not know the command to call up information, nothing would happen. Once the commands were learned there was a lot of information available to the staff member. The SENTRY terminals were supposed to be staff only access.

The SENTRY system used what were called dumb terminals. The keyboard was the command processor. The real computer was at a central location. The assigned printer was a daisy wheel printer and was very, very, slow. It was the state of the art at the time.

In the control room it took nearly 6 hours of the 8 hour shift to print out the work rosters and the master inmate information roster for the institution. As the years progressed new terminals would be added to the system and

147

a faster dot matrix printer was added. Each device had to have a coax cable ran to it. The main controller for the system was located in the tunnel below the control room.

When I was the control room officer, I used to send staff into the tunnel to reset the controller when it would go off line. For years I would describe exactly what the procedure was to reset the controller.

It was not until about 1997 when I became a computer specialist for the prison did I ever go to the tunnel and see the controller. I had read the instruction sheet I was provided on how to troubleshoot the system when SENTRY was down. I maintained a lot of computer and SENTRY information in my control room officer's hand book.

After the computer network was installed at the prison, the SENTRY system access was being placed on each computer, I became the single point of contact for all access for SENTRY and the sensitive information access levels. I also became a National Criminal Information Center (NCIC) coordinator for law enforcement information system access. We had to maintain the certification for the system access as a user and administrator. I also coordinated visitor clearance and access to the institution.

At the federal prison camp there was an electronics vocational class. That classroom, had about a dozen computers set up, and the inmates that were enrolled in the class had unlimited access to the computers and the programming for the computers. One of the first applications that came out of the classroom was an inmate visiting program. After a while security concerns about inmate access to computers, lead to more restrictions being placed on the inmates.

WALKING MAINLINE

In the vocational training section of the education department inmates they were limited in use of computers. The inmates were not allowed to program computers. They were instructed on how to use word processing programs, spread sheets and limited data base programs. The education department had a staff member who directly supervised the inmates on computers. The federal prison industries business office allowed inmates to perform billing and material tracking on inmate computers in the business office.

Inmate computer systems were installed on a different type of network than the network used by staff. Inmates were screened for computer access as computer "Yes" or computer "No." Inmates were not supposed to be allowed on staff computers. Software security programs were to be installed on inmate access computers.

I learned to be a SENTRY expert when I was in correctional services. During some of the shifts when the times were slow I would read the SENTRY procedures manual and practice the commands on a SENTRY terminal that I had access to. Some of the shift lieutenants would challenge the control room offices on information searches we would conduct on the SENTRY system. It was not often that we could be stumped over a SENTRY related question.

It was during one of my morning watch shifts in control that a major security problem concerning certain very sensitive information was discovered in the SENTRY system. This was reported to one of the coordinators for SENTRY. The central office was provided the information and the problem was resolved. We both were given awards for this work.

WALKING MAINLINE

When I was working control, I put together a handbook for the control room officers. The book was a guide for the officer so they could produce on demand rosters or a listing for the escorting officer's information about the inmate they would be responsible for escorting outside the prison.

One of the information packets contained medical information that the local hospital would require when an inmate was admitted for treatment. Other packets concerned custody and security information on the inmate. There was a duty officer packet. Much of that information was adopted nationwide for other prisons to use.

There was a training packet developed for the special investigative supervisors. This training packet had every search template that could be used on most SENTRY terminals. This was a resource that was very valuable for gaining inmate information. The lieutenant that assembled the packet took many, many hours to run and refine the rosters. The commands were common to the system, but setup in a way that it just demonstrated how much information was available in the data base if the terminal operator just knew how to send out the inquiry.

A SENTRY terminal operator used to be able to send what was called a "Switch Message." We could send text messages to a screen at a SENTRY terminal. The messages could be almost anything you could write. I used to warn people that we had to be professional and not use profane language.

I learned a trick that you could send a signal to the SENTRY printer in control that made the printer sound like a body alarm. I only did it one time and that was with a lieutenant's permission. He wanted to test a new control room officer, on how he would react in a stressful situation.

WALKING MAINLINE

During one Christmas Eve shift, when things were very slow, just after 6:00 P.M., I was sending out a switch message to the control room officer on duty inside the penitentiary. My assignment was the camp officer in charge and acting camp lieutenant. The message sent was that I had caught a camper named "Chris Kringle" A.K.A. "Santa Claus" in an off limit's area at the federal prison camp.

I reported he was in a sleigh with eight tiny reindeer, and was dressed in a red suit with white trim. He had a long white beard. He had a belly that when he laughed, it shook like a bowl full of jelly. His sleigh was filled with gift packages wrapped in Christmas paper, he had toys and other stuff in the sleigh.

In the report we had not determined if the items were stolen property. Worse yet it was discovered he was on escape status. He was tested with our breathalyzer and he blew a .20 indicating he was intoxicated. I had him locked in our detention cage. I asked the control room officer if they had room at the penitentiary to place this guy in the special housing unit.

In the message I stated that he was yelling very loud and when he was placed in hand cuffs he insisted that he had to get on his way to deliver the sleigh full of presents.

I asked the question if any staff were available to help inventory all the property and what was going to be done with eight tiny reindeer, because they were filling our yard with reindeer manure.

Okay, it was a pretty slow night. Well the control room officer had not only routed my message to the control printer, he routed it to the operations lieutenant and to every penitentiary in the bureau of prisons. That pretty much ended a slow shift. Each control room officer along with the shift lieutenants added to the message with their own answers to my request for assistance.

Each penitentiary offered their special operations response team, bus crews, and property officers to help with the inventory. A response was made with a further update on the status of the inmate and how amazing it was that when we started to inventory the property that "Chris Kringle" had in the sleigh the pile was growing larger and we were running out of room. It was also added that we put the reindeer in a temporary cattle pen and the manure was just piling up something awful.

The penitentiary control officer and I were busy responding on the SENTRY terminal to all the message traffic. The central office SENTRY operator got into the act and he switched the message traffic to all available SENTRY terminals. To say the least we got really busy.

Generally during the holiday we would have an 8:00 P.M. count. The camp inmates would sit on the bunks until the officers counted the unit. I looked at the clock and realized we were about an hour late for the count.

Both myself and the penitentiary control room officer ended the messages we started since we had to do count. The inmates were patiently waiting on the bunks when we did the count. We combined the count and that was the end of the SENTRY "Santa Claus" as an escaped inmate story. It was one of the few times that the control room officers did this sort of thing with the SENTRY terminals.

As a correctional officer just a few of us had access to SENTRY information. When I retired, we were teaching staff on how to access SENTRY information. Since most computers had SENTRY access, training was made available in a classroom.

A command list was available to any staff member. The list was organized into groups of commands that staff assigned to various duty positions could use. The SENTRY user manual used to be listed as a sensitive document and restricted in its use, that designation has now changed.

Unit management is one of the largest users of the SENTRY system.

Chapter 19

DRUGS

Excerpts from the:

Semiannual Report to Congress
October 1, 2002–March 31, 2003
Office of the Inspector General (OIG)

THE FEDERAL BUREAU OF PRISONS
The BOP operates a nationwide system of prisons and detention facilities to incarcerate and detain inmates who have been imprisoned for federal crimes or are awaiting trial or sentencing in federal court. The BOP consists of approximately 36,000 employees, 102 institutions, six regional offices, two staff training centers, and 29 community corrections offices. The BOP is responsible for the custody and care of approximately 163,000 federal offenders, 137,500 of whom are confined in BOP-operated correctional institutions and detention centers. The remainder are confined in detention centers, privately operated prisons, community corrections centers, juvenile facilities, and facilities operated by state or local governments.

REPORTS ISSUED
THE BOP'S DRUG INTERDICTION ACTIVITIES
In this review, the OIG evaluated whether the BOP has been effective in reducing or eliminating drugs in BOP institutions. We found that drugs are widespread in BOP institutions even though the BOP implements interdiction

155

activities at most entry points in its institutions. Inmates' positive drug tests, misconduct charges, and overdoses show drug use and drug smuggling occur in almost every BOP institution. The OIG identified inmate visitors, staff, and mail as the three primary ways drugs enter BOP institutions. The OIG found that the BOP fails to search visitors adequately and that most of the BOP institutions the OIG visited have insufficient cameras, monitors, and staff to adequately supervise inmate visiting sessions.

The OIG also determined that the BOP imposes no restrictions on the personal property staff can bring into its institutions, does not search staff or their property when they enter for duty, and does not conduct random drug testing of staff, such activities are common in many state correctional systems. At each BOP institution the OIG visited, staff brought in duffle bags, briefcases, satchels, and large and small coolers.

Institution managers, intelligence officers, and correctional officers interviewed by the OIG expressed serious doubt about the effectiveness of the BOP's efforts to eliminate drugs from its institutions when it imposes no control over the property its staff brings inside.

In addition, the OIG found that the BOP does not conduct random drug tests of its staff despite having won a federal court case in 1993 to permit such testing and despite a written BOP policy that requires drug testing. The majority of BOP staff interviewed by the OIG supported random drug testing of staff.

The review also examined the BOP's efforts to reduce inmates' demand for drugs. The OIG found that an insufficient number of BOP inmates receive drug treatment, partly because the BOP underestimates and inadequately tracks inmates' treatment needs. The BOP has estimated that 34 percent of all federal inmates need drug treatment. However, the OIG concluded that this figure is outdated and under represents the number of BOP inmates who need drug treatment.

In addition, the OIG concluded that the BOP does not provide adequate nonresidential drug treatment in BOP facilities because of insufficient staffing, lack of policy guidance, and lack of incentives for inmates to seek drug treatment. Even though the BOP states that nonresidential treatment is a major component of its strategy to reduce inmates' demand for drugs, nonresidential treatment was limited or not available at five of the institutions the OIG visited.

The OIG made 15 recommendations to improve the BOP's drug interdiction efforts.

End of excerpt

For a while at the penitentiary we had drug dog teams. A dog handler and the assigned K-9 were trained as a team to locate drugs within the penitentiary and on the prison grounds. The prison also utilized the K-9 teams from local law enforcement and the U. S. Air Force base. The dog teams were kept pretty busy.

Were a lot of drugs found inside the penitentiary? I really don't know. I do know I responded to several incidents of drug overdose. I had one case where the inmate had grand mal seizures and the cause of his death was determined to be a drug overdose.

Naloxone is a drug used to counter the effects of a heroin or morphine overdose. Naloxone is specifically used to counteract life-threatening depression of the central nervous system and respiratory system. It is marketed under the trademark Narcan.

I was training a new correctional officer and giving him a tour of my unit. I was assigned as the correctional counselor for "L" Lincoln unit. The operations lieutenant had sent a new correctional officer for some training and a tour of a housing unit. As the officer and I were walking the unit he asked me how to search a cell if an inmate was sleeping in the cell. I told him let us find a cell with an inmate sleeping in his bunk. We walked down "B" range of the unit and found a cell where the inmate was asleep. I shook the foot of the inmate to wake him up. I learned it was safer to shake the foot to wake an inmate rather than touching a shoulder to wake them from sleeping.

The inmate got up out of his bed, we searched him and I directed him to go to the front of the unit and wait. The practice of sending an inmate to the front of the unit was to insure the inmate was away from the cell during a cell search. This was for officer safety.

We started the cell search, dividing the cell into three levels. We looked at the top level, then the middle level and finally the lower level. When the inmates locker was opened we found on the middle shelf five small round packages just slightly smaller than a golf ball wrapped in a clear plastic. It looked like black tar heroin.

The officer took the packages to the lieutenant's office for testing. The inmate was also escorted to the lieutenant's office. The unit officer secured the cell door. A few minutes later a telephone call from the lieutenant's office informed us the test was positive for narcotics and to secure the inmate's property. The lieutenant was told that I would write the supporting memo for the officer's incident report and we would get the inmates property secured.

The inmate was holding the narcotics for another inmate in the unit. The drugs had been smuggled into the prison that very day. The officer was given credit for the bust and a special act award of a couple of a hundred dollars for the find. It was a good lesson on how to conduct a cell search.

Several inmates selected me to be a staff representative for them before the disciplinary hearing officer (DHO). The DHO hears higher level cases for the inmates when they violate the inmate disciplinary codes. The process is much like a criminal court process but is administrative in nature and generally takes place before formal court actions.

Inmates who were charged with narcotics use because of positive results of a urine test would go before the DHO. The standard for a finding that an inmate had committed a prohibited act was some evidence. It is not the same standard as in a criminal court. The inmates wanted me to show to the DHO, that BOP policy was not followed when the urine was collected.

It was true the policy statement was not followed by staff in the collection and processing of the urine samples. The chain of custody would be violated. I would bring this to the attention of the DHO and the charges would be dismissed. This did not make me popular with the correctional staff.

What was worked out as a solution to this problem of not following policy, the procedure was changed to document on how the urine specimen was collected, tagged as evidence, and processed.

After a positive report was returned on an inmate, medical records were reviewed and it was documented by the medical officer that the inmate was not prescribed the narcotic. This process insured a finding that could not be overturned on appeal of the case.

This change in procedures resulted in a better process for drug use detection. The rewriting of the local policy helped to insure compliance with national policy. After a while I was not being selected as a staff representative.

Quite a few times staff responded to what was an inmate drug overdose. One case we responded to an inmate drug overdose in "F" unit during morning work call. The inmate was having grand mal seizures in his cell. He was removed from the cell and he was taken to the prison hospital emergency room. Narcan was administered but there was little effect. I was the officer in charge of the escorted trip to the local hospital.

When we arrived at the hospital we were referred for transfer to another hospital. That hospital had MRI equipment and an advanced emergency room. The inmate was having major convulsions and seizures. His body temperatures varied from chills to high fever. The brain scan indicated a small cerebral hemorrhage that grew from thumb nail size to the size of a baseball within a short time. This was killing him.

My shift ended at 4:00 P.M., and the inmate was still having major convulsions and seizures. My relief arrived and I went home. The inmate died about two hours later.

It was some time later we responded to a call for assistance in the prison laundry room. When staff arrived on scene an inmate was down on the floor. He was barely breathing and not responsive. He was placed on a hospital gurney and transported to the emergency room. It looked like he was dead. The hospital physician's assistant gave the inmate an injection of Narcan. In less than five minutes the inmate was, sitting up, breathing normally, and was alive. The inmate was not happy that his "high" was taken away. Based upon the treatment by the hospital staff the inmate received an incident report for unauthorized use of narcotics and placed in detention.

One of my last times of responding to a drug overdose was to the federal prison industries cable factory. It is a long run out to the factory area and transporting an inmate to the prison hospital takes a few minutes. Narcan brought the inmate back. Staff response to an incident is fast and if needed inmates can be transported to a local medical facility rapidly.

Chapter 20

EDUCATION

The penitentiary at Lompoc has an inmate education department. Several job training courses were available to inmates. The dental vocational training program provided training where inmates could complete the course of instruction and become very proficient in the making of dentures and other related dental prosthesis. Passing the certification exam was the goal of this program.

The barber vocational training program was available, and in this program an inmate could become a licensed barber. The federal prison camp had a vocational meat processing program. There was a solder certification program for precision electronic soldering. There were other programs an inmate could take advantage of if they were so inclined. The computer vocational training program did not allow computer programming but the inmates could learn how to use word processing and spread sheet applications. The GED program was available. English as a second language was offered in the classroom. Several college courses were offered.

The education department also had a legal library for inmate use in the legal appeal process or to file complaints in federal district court. A federal civil court case could not go on without the administrative remedy process being exhausted by the inmate first.

The education department could be a very busy place. Inmates were more behaved in this department than in other areas of the prison.

Chapter 21

FEMALES

When I first started working at the penitentiary in 1985 there were no female correctional officers. Female correctional officers were at lower level institutions. We had a female correctional counselor at the federal prison camp.

Inside the penitentiary when a female staff member walked the main corridor a male staff member performed escort duty. It was not meant to be demeaning or anything like that. It was a courtesy, just like holding a door open for a woman to go through or pulling out a chair at a table when a woman was going to be seated. You could call it the old time treatment of women. It was a sign of respect.

Around 1990 or so the penitentiary had hired and placed on duty female correctional officers. Custody or correctional services was still a pretty "Macho" department. The men in custody act different with women just like in any organization with a male dominance.

When females first started to work units and correctional posts I was asked what I thought of the situation. I expressed my feelings, a staff member is a staff member, all I ask is if a call for assistance is made then staff respond. I did not care if the staff were male or female, just do the job.

I was on duty during the evening shift as a correctional counselor in "J" Joker unit. This unit was designated as the "UNICOR" or prison industry inmate housing unit. Inmates housed in this unit worked in UNICOR.

From inside the office I heard a trash can being kicked around outside the door. There were sounds like an inmate fight outside the officer's station. I quickly responded to what turned out to be an inmate who was mad because the female unit officer had performed a pat down search of him.

The officer had recovered some contraband from the inmate and the inmate wanted to argue with the officer. A crowd of inmates was forming. There appeared to be a couple of dozen inmates that were going to jump into the argument.

I stepped between the officer and inmate, the inmate was told I wanted to talk to him outside the unit in the main corridor. I then walked the inmate to the front entrance door and out into the corridor.

There were three or four officers waiting. They had responded to the noise coming from the unit. I told the inmate to turn around, put his hands on the wall and I was going to search him. The inmate made the statement "I am going to the hole, ain't I?" I told him I was taking him to the lieutenant's office then to the hole.

I had a couple of the officers go into the unit and check on the status of the unit. The inmates had gone back to normal activity. The inmate was escorted to the operations lieutenant's office, then to the detention unit.

I returned to "J" unit and talked with the new officer. She told me she had the situation under control. I explained to her the inmate was being placed in detention for attempted assault on staff, refusing an order, and insolence toward staff.

I asked her to write the incident report and told her I would write the supporting memo. I told her it did not matter to me who the officer was that had a problem with the inmate. Having the inmate close to the front door and walking him out into the main corridor away from the other inmates solved several problems. The inmate did not have to put up a show for the other inmates, he could be controlled better out in the corridor since other staff were responding to the noise.

No inmate should resist a search, refuse an order, attempt to assault staff, and possibly cause a disturbance. We had solved the problem with the least amount of force and allowed the inmate to "Save face." It was a good lesson for common correctional sense.

For the most part female staff did not perform strip searches of inmates. It was good to have female correctional staff to conduct visitor searches of females.

It took some getting used to for the penitentiary inmates to behave with female correctional staff. During counts and other routine times in a unit the inmates had to remember female staff were working the unit. There were times female officers would see inmates taking a shower, which was not too much of a problem since it became routine as long as the inmate did not misbehave.

I was on duty in control during a day watch shift. I received a telephone call from the education department. The education secretary had informed me an inmate had masturbated in front of her. I called the main corridor over to the control room key slot window and told him what had happened.

He took couple of officers with him to pick up the inmate. He and the other officers responded not at a run but a quick pace. They entered the education department, cuffed, and escorted the inmate to the operations lieutenant's office.

When the inmate was cuffed in front of the other inmates in the department, his zipper was still unzipped, and he was exposed. He was walked out of the office and down the corridor to be placed in detention.

After the inmate was locked up I called the secretary and told her she needed to write the incident report. I told her the inmate was placed in detention. She did thank me for the rapid response to her call and not making it a major event.

I also informed her when the report was processed and if the inmate was found to have committed a prohibited act, he would be placed on a watch list as a sexual predator. This would be part of his permanent record.

I told her she might want to call her husband who worked at the penitentiary and tell him what happened. He later thanked me for being a professional in doing my job.

I found in my dealings with female correctional staff, a female officer sometimes could handle a situation better than a male officer. I also tried not to treat female officers any different from a male officer.

I worked with a couple of female officers who later became lieutenants, one a correctional counselor, and one became an associate warden. All of them highly qualified as managers and supervisors.

I worked with a female correctional officer that was on video tape when an inmate assaulted another inmate with a knife in front of her. The officer working the unit across from hers had responded to the assault. He was unable to call for assistance.

On the video tape it appeared she was running from the situation when in fact, after the tape was reviewed, she was calling for assistance in order for additional staff to respond to the assault.

WALKING MAINLINE

She was one of the officers who were on duty in the video room when an officer was killed in our main corridor. She had seen the event live on the video monitor. She had to rerun the video tape of the killing many times for the FBI and other investigative staff. She later became a lieutenant at another facility.

About a year or so after I retired, I met the first female warden for the Federal Correctional Complex at Lompoc. She was standing in line at the local post office. I walked up to her and told her "You too with only one hour of correctional training can work at the United States Penitentiary Lompoc," she did look at me like I was just a little crazy.

I introduced myself and told her I had retired after 21 years working at the penitentiary. I worked in computer services. She told me that she had heard of me. We talked a few minutes about how things were going at the prison.

She told me a limited number of US Penitentiary Lompoc Christmas souvenir ornaments were available and asked if I wanted one. I asked to have one saved for me so I could pick it up the next day. Later that afternoon, a call was placed to her secretary to arrange for a time to pick up the ornament.

One of the best unit secretaries in the world worked on our unit team. I know she had to put up with a lot from me and the case manager that I worked with for several years. We made a very good unit team. She went from unit management to the warden's staff. She is a really great worker. Her mother worked at the penitentiary and had retired.

We had a couple of female correctional officers who resigned from the bureau because of inappropriate behavior with inmates. Stuff happens.

Chapter 22

FOOD SERVICE

To me working food service either as a staff member or inmate is just not a great job. Three times a day a meal must be served. This is a total of 1700 meals each time. Almost 400 meals or so are for the special housing units and must be loaded into portable food carts, kept hot, transported to the special housing unit, and served by staff to each inmate housed in the unit.

Serving the general population in a mess hall designed for 650 inmates is a tough job and a real accomplishment. The prison population was over 1650 inmates. Many times the food service department is taken for granted. Standing steam line to supervise the inmates or standing the wall to listen to inmate complaints is not the most pleasant job there is.

Most of the inmates assigned to food service do not like having to work in food service. For a few of the inmates they like working as a cook or in the bakery. The food service work day starts at 3:00 A.M. The work day will end at about 7:00 P.M. after clean up and all the food service items are put in storage.

The food service warehouse contains all the food for at least three days. There are walk-in coolers and a knife room where inmates are issued knives for performing the carving and cutting in food preparation.

Each shift foreman has a break out cage assigned for his, breakfast, lunch, and dinner meal. In that cage are all the items that are necessary for preparation of that shift. Cold storage items are listed and set aside for the shift. At least in theory it is.

During a lock down, staff are selected to prepare the hundreds of sandwiches and bag lunches to feed the inmates locked in the cells. Most staff do not like being assigned to this duty.

A small officers mess was opened for staff meals. Generally what inmates are served on the food service main line is the same meal is served to staff. The meal rates are reasonable.

The staffing assignments for the food service department were: a food service administrator, an assistant food service administrator, a segregation food cart foreman, a food cook foreman for each shift and at least one other food service foreman for each shift. There also was a bakery foreman. Food service staff are on a really good pay scale.

For a time I was assigned as the acting assistant food service administrator when we were short food service staff. It was a day watch shift. I did a lot of running around. I had to control the issue of yeast, and sensitive items.

My set of keys opened storage areas that were restricted to staff and I issued food items that had to be controlled. During the meals I had to insure everything was ready for the cook foreman.

During my first week on the job I had a meeting with the inmate crews in the mess hall. I told the inmate crews they could not take anything from the mess hall that general population inmates could not have. The inmates could not issue extra food to their friends. There were told to show up on time and do their work.

172

WALKING MAINLINE

The number one job was mainline food serving. The inmates were told when mainline was finished for the general population there would be a seconds line. Left over food would be issued at that time and it did not matter how much anyone ate. The mainline had to be served first. If the inmate crews could not follow the rules, stole food, or did not want to work, they would escorted personally to the detention unit.

The inmates were shown my issued handcuffs and they talked among themselves saying, yes I would take them to the "hole." My reputation among the inmates was I would do as I told them. There were only one or two inmates that were placed in detention because of any problems.

It was a very happy time for me when my tour in food service ended and staffing for the department had improved. The food service administrator was one of the best and he demanded a good product at a fair price from the vendors.

According to food service industry reports in 1998 food cost ran $2.49 per day per inmate in the federal system. To me was pretty amazing to be able to feed inmates at this rate.

Chapter 23

General Activities Center

The area known as the General Activities Center (G.A.C.) was located on the second floor above the visiting corridor of the penitentiary. It housed several inmate groups. It also was the location when the Federal Parole Commission Board met to hold hearings on old law inmates. We also called the place "Gang Activities Center."

The various groups that met in the center were the Tribe of Five Feathers (TOFF), an American Indian Group, Italian American Club, Lompoc Prison Writers Club and several other meeting groups.

The writer's club had inmates who wanted to write books, movie scripts, or just write stories. The inmates could not conduct a business or be paid while in prison. They would gather on a regular basis to discuss current projects. Various book authors, Hollywood script writers, and other personalities would visit from time to time.

One of the more famous persons who visited was Gene Roddenberry of the television series "Star Trek." A few movie stars and stunt players did visit the prison.

Anthony Hopkins, a movie star, and Ridley Scott a Hollywood director visited the penitentiary for research about the prison.

The G.A.C. was later converted for use by the religious services department. This was in additional to the chapel area that was inside the penitentiary.

Chapter 24

INFORMANTS

The "snitch" game as some people called it, was not really for me. To me the term "snitch," was just not a good term to use. A lot of times inmates would provide or trade information for favors. I said and told the inmates I did not play the "snitch" game. I wanted to know what was going on in the prison.

The concern was for my safety first, staff safety second, and inmate safety third. I also said at times this concern would be the same across the board, my job was safety, security, and accountability.

My comment to the inmates was, "My job was to catch them and their job was to try and get away with stuff."

I knew I would lose since I did not have 24/7 to think of ideas to get away with.

I treated informants as an information resource. I would listen to what was being said and then check out the information. I must admit I am an information junkie.

Developing good informants is an art. Some people have a natural skill on having people tell them things. Then it becomes what do you do with the information?

I was able to develop a very large network of informants and information resources. Staff and inmates spread rumors and we all talk.

One of the first times I had developed a reliable and tested informant in the prison I was called into the special investigative supervisor's office. It was demanded that I provide the inmate's name.

According to policy at the time we were not required to register an informant. What was required that a memo be written concerning the reliability of the information provided by the inmate in the past. I had several concerns about having to lose a good informant and did not want to share him.

I told the investigator it would be simple, I would appear in a federal district court judge's chambers for an "in camera" hearing and provide the judge the name of the informant. I would explain how I tested the reliability of the informant. Then the judge would determine if the name would be released. I left the office with the investigator mad at me, but I was not bothered about the issue again.

There were times way too much information would be coming through the informant network to keep up with. Writing memo's to document and check out the information took up a lot of time.

A few times the rumor would be about a certain inmate who would be on a hit list. The inmates had access to a unit mail box in which outgoing mail could be placed.

Notes would be dropped in that box, I called the notes "Snow Flakes." At times there would be a dozen of these notes written by different inmates about a certain inmate was going to be beaten up, killed, or otherwise harmed. This was serious business and that information was passed on immediately.

Correctional counselors would have notes and other information slid under the office door concerning what was happening from informants. If something was going down immediately, the notes would be slid under the unit officer's door.

A work site or staff member supervising an inmate work crew would be told information that would not be shared anywhere else. Working with an inmate crew on a daily basis, a lot of information is shared by the inmates with the staff.

A simple statement from an inmate like "You have a man down on the flats," can lead to finding an inmate that is murdered or injured.

Informants will also trade information for favors. When staff who are committing actions against policy or illegal, inmates can use trade information to get favors or special consideration.

All staff have to do to stay out of trouble is follow policy and do no wrong. If staff are professional in the prison, on and off the job, then there is no problem.

There was one inmate informant I wanted to see how well he was plugged into the information network. I told him, I had heard a certain associate warden had been selected as warden. The associate warden was not well liked and not likely to be selected as a warden.

In less than an hour, telephone calls were coming into the prison from our central office in Washington, D.C., with the question how did this associate warden become a warden? It was amazing how this rumor went out so fast and so far. It confirmed on how well the inmate was connected to his information network.

Escape plots and plans for escapes were always in circulation. A few times when the information was checked by staff the escape was in progress. Rumors of tunnels were always going around the prison. Staff would go and check out the rumor.

WALKING MAINLINE

According to one rumor, it was said a tunnel was being dug near our inside print plant. The building was next to the recreation yard. A staff member was told to check out the story. He was walking around the outside of the building when he fell into a hole that was in the middle of the tunnel. The rumor had checked out.

When I was an officer working a housing unit. I had heard a certain inmate was gambling and losing his bets. He had an arrogant attitude. He was told generally if inmate could not pay their bills a warning message would be given them. First it was against policy for inmates to gamble. He was told there was a concern about my safety, about staff safety, then about inmate safety.

If an inmate was not paying his bills the first warning he could get was a beating or he would be thumped. The second warning could be he would be piped or beaten with a pool stick. The third warning may be a stabbing or the inmate could be killed.

I did my memo about what I was told about the inmate from my informants. About a week or so later that same inmate was piped in the head, and the assault had occurred in the unit game room. He was placed in protective custody.

I talked with the inmate when he was in the lock down unit. He told me he did not believe me when he was told about getting in trouble gambling. He was more than a thousand dollars in debt. The inmate was reminded it was against policy to gamble. After recovering from head wounds he was transferred to another prison for his protection.

WALKING MAINLINE

I was working a housing unit during my second year. It was during an evening watch shift, when I was told by one of the unit inmates that an event called the "Village Games" was going on.

I had walked around the unit on a regular basis. Walking the unit was a means for me to find out what was happening, to conduct cell searches, and just to keep awake.

Most of the time things did not seem out of the ordinary. The inmates would be playing cards in the third tier card room and it seemed normal activity in the remainder of the unit.

It was during one of my rounds in the unit I saw a "Jigger," this is an inmate who stands lookout and tells the other inmates "Man Walking" as a warning that the officer was nearby.

I was walking on the second tier while the look out was on the third tier, I reversed my walk when the inmate was not looking, and came up the stairway to the third tier. I stood at the door way of the inmate card room.

The room had about a dozen inmates sitting around the card table playing cards. The inmates in the room tried to hide money that was in the form of coins, chips, and markers under the table cover. I asked them what kind of card game they were playing. The inmates told me they were playing pinochle.

I joked a little bit with them and asked the question, "If an inmate had six aces was that a problem?" Then I laughed and told them I was only kidding. I told them to have a good game and left to finish my rounds of the unit.

When I returned to my office I started to make a list of names of the inmates in the card game.

I used the inmate 5x8 housing cards to make positive identification of the inmates in the card room. It looked like a poker game was going on. A while later one of the inmates approached me and told me, "Thank You" on how I handled the situation. I told the inmate it looked like they were just playing cards.

During my rounds for the next week or so I saw who was running the dice games and who appeared to be in charge of the whole "Village Games" gambling operation.

One of the items of information the special investigative lieutenant was looking for was who kept the books and markers in this gambling operation. It took a couple of days but I found out which inmate was holding the books and IOU markers. An extensive memo was written on what was discovered.

It was during my 2 days off when the major players and inmates running the gambling operation were locked up. Later the FBI charged several of the inmates with gambling crimes. The amount of money involved, was in the thousands of dollars. Finding the stash of books and betting markers was the key to the enforcement operation.

It was during a day watch shift, while working as main corridor officer, I received information that an inmate in "L" Lincoln unit was dealing drugs in a cell on E range.

I sent an officer to check out the rumor. The officer arrived at the cell during an activity's movement. The inmates in the cell, in an attempt to get out and not get caught with drugs, almost knocked the officer over the three story high railing. The officer then called for assistance and staff responded.

It was after that incident when I was informed by the operations lieutenant, the next time that an officer was going to check out something like that, it needed to cleared with him first.

Correctional counselors can build a very large network on inmate informants. A work site supervisor can also have fairly reliable informants.

Sometimes an inmate will ask if a certain staff member is reliable or can be trusted. Depending on the situation a judgment call has to be made.

In one case an inmate informant asked me that question about a certain staff member. I told the inmate yes that staff member could be trusted. It turned out to be a major case was developed with the informant.

I did not care who got the credit for the information. The goal was for the information to be useful. Inmate informants are a tool of the trade.

False information provided by informants is always present. Sometimes in order to get staff in trouble false reports are made about staff. This is where careful investigation and checking out the information takes place. Information on staff is closely held. The information is either true, partly true, or false. Inmates like to see staff scramble and chase dead end rumors. To the inmate it was a game.

Staff have been known to provide false information on inmates to get the inmate in trouble. I always said if you watch the inmates long enough they would give themselves away and get caught. Staff did not have to set up any inmate.

The phrase to "Play it straight" is used. This is being honest and direct in dealing with inmates and inmate informants.

To me protection of an information resource was important. Mishandling informant information can get the source injured or killed.

It is also important to treat everyone the same and not reveal an informant by your actions. Always listen and check out the information.

Staff informants can cause a problem in how to handle the information. When you are a witness to an event and you are required to report it, well then report it. It is when you don't report it you can get into trouble. You must use discretion in how you treat information. Don't create or try to embellish, you see something that is wrong, then you have to deal with it. Also use what is called common sense in a correctional environment.

Chapter 25

INMATE HOUSING UNITS

I used to think it would be an easy task to house inmates in a prison. Just point out an empty bunk and tell the inmate here is your bed and locker for personal items. Well in real life it did not work that way. The penitentiary had several different housing units when I started working there.

We had "B" unit, an outside cell block with cells almost like rooms. No sinks or toilets in the cell and a common shower. The other very unusual thing about the unit was the inmates had keys to the cell doors. When I first saw this, I had remarked why did we not just give the inmates keys to the front gate. I was told "Don't be a smart ass."

"B" unit was not manned 24/7, in fact the unit officer shift was from 2:00 P.M. to 10:00 P.M. to cover count and even then the post was not always manned. A telephone was mounted outside the office for inmate use during emergencies. It was tied into the "222" triple duce emergency system. It was a couple of years before this was changed and a unit officer was assigned 24/7 for the unit.

Another unusual housing unit was "D" and "E" units. These two units were open dorm units. In a penitentiary this was a very different way to house inmates.

"C," "F," "J," "K," and "L," units were outside cell houses. This means the cells were along the outside of the cell block and there was a center floor area called "The flats" and this was the first floor.

"H" unit was a center block unit, that is the cells were in the center of the unit with no connection to the outside walls.

"H" unit was designated as a quiet unit. No loud shouting or noise was allowed. The officer would walk the tiers as quietly as possible and would try not to rattle the keys. The quiet unit designation was for a couple of reasons. One reason was the inmates assigned to the unit were high escape risks. The quiet designation was made to insure the officer could hear digging or the sound of metal scraping on cement. Another reason was the unit team wanted it as quiet as possible without the noise of a regular housing unit.

"I" unit was in two parts, upper "I" and lower "I." The unit was also called the "Hole." It was the detention and disciplinary unit. Lower "I" had what could be called "Box Car" cells. There was an inside sliding metal grill. The outside door was a solid steel door with a small window in it. The outside door could be closed and the lights turned off to make the cell quite dark. Only the most dangerous and assaultive inmates would be placed in these cells. One cell was a legal resource center. There were only about 16 or 17 cells in lower "I." Upper "I" unit was two tiers high with a range of cells designated as disciplinary cells and the remainder of the cells were administrative detention cells.

"M" unit was the US Marshal's holdover unit. The inmates assigned to this housing unit were waiting transfer to other prisons. This was during the time with the BOP operated an inmate bus fleet, that was used to transport inmates from prison to prison across the nation. This was before the US Marshal's airline transportation service.

A unit officer would receive an inmate into his unit. The inmate would have a 5x8 housing card, and the card was handled by staff only. The card had information about the inmate, his name, number, and other identifying data. On the back of the card confidential notes about the inmate behavior or other information that staff should know about the inmate was entered. The front of the card would include custody information and what security level the inmate was.

The unit officer would assign an inmate to a cell that was designed by the unit team. The conditions of cell assignments would be based upon race, possible prison gang affiliation, custody and other factors that would be taken into consideration for inmate management.

Inmates that were white could be housed with Asian, Hispanic, or other white inmates. It would be rare that a black inmate was housed with a white inmate. Asian and Hispanic inmates could be housed with white inmates or black inmates.

The housing cards would be arranged in the same order as the cell block was set up. When inmates had a change of cell assignment or were assigned outside the unit, the housing card would have to be changed or follow the inmate.

A housing locator book was also used in the unit to insure accountability of inmates assigned to that unit. When an inmate arrived to the unit or left the unit the officer would call control to update the base count of the unit, make the changes in the unit log book, change the housing card, and update the locator book.

This had to be done every time any changes to inmate quarters assignments were made. The control room officer had a similar job in the control room to perform for maintaining inmate accountability.

When an inmate was placed in detention, the officer also had to secure the inmate's cell and personal property.

Inmates were issued metal lockers to store personal property. A locker measured about 3 feet high, 18 inches deep, and almost 2 feet wide. The lockers were furnished with round metal rods or flat metal bars to provide a locking mechanism for the door. A change to the lockers had to be made. The rods and bars were being made into "Shanks," prison knives made by the inmates, so they had to be removed from the lockers before being issued to the inmates. A metal hasp was installed and a combination lock was used to secure the locker.

For years the penitentiary had all single cells. This changed around 1990 when both the new federal criminal law took affect, the Washington, D.C. correctional system shipped the overflow of inmates to the prisons, and the Cuban riots.

Double bunks were added in the prison to about half of a housing unit. For example before the double cells, a unit would hold 120 inmates, after the bunks were added the capacity was increased to 180 inmates with 60 cells being converted to double bunks.

The cell doors in several of the units were opened by a drum and roller system that was located at the end of each tier. This was a round drum that would be turned and a lever moved to an open or closed position to open and close a cell door.

Other units had a large lever located in a lock box at the end of each tier that would be pulled to release the cell doors. The unit officer in some units would have to key each cell door to allow the door to open or be closed and locked. This would require a lot of fast walking on the part of the officer to open and close cell doors at count time. The inmates would have to cooperate by holding the doors closed in order to secure the unit. When all the cell doors were locked, the officer would pull on each of the doors to insure the door was secure. More than a few times a cell door would not be secured when the officer checked the door.

The only unit that had the electrically operated doors was "L" unit. These doors were operated from a large electrical panel inside a lock box located at the front end of each of the tiers in the unit. The main box was on the left hand side of the unit. The doors could be remotely opened and closed. It worked well when there was electrical power. When power was out, the doors had to be operated manually.

After a few years, all the cell block doors were converted to electrical doors. When the power to the prison worked so did the doors. When the power was off, it was manual operation of the doors.

The dorm units were the only units that had metal grills to the unit and did not have doors for inmate cells. The units were closed in 2005 or so. A new special housing unit was built to replace these housing units. These old units were torn down.

The old federal prison camp had both dorm units were open bays and six man rooms. When the camp was upgraded to a federal correctional institution, the housing units changed. The boot camp and new federal prison camp have open bay housing units.

The unit officer or federal prison camp officers had to insure the locator books were up to date and that inmates did not move on their own in the housing units.

In the penitentiary a single cell waiting list assignment on our SENTRY computer system was created. This was used for a waiting list inmates were placed on in chronological order for assignment to a single cell. Before the creation of this list unit correctional counselors kept a single cell waiting list by several means.

One problem developed during this period was inmates would sell their spot on the waiting list to the highest bidder. This practice ended with the computer assignment system.

In 1987 the new federal drug sentencing laws took effect. These laws provided for longer sentences and limited good time for inmates to 54 days a year. The old law inmates could be released by the US Parole Commission parole boards with extra good time earned. This kept the inmate population lower in the federal system. The old time inmate was a different kind of inmate.

The new law inmates were more disruptive and caused more problems with housing assignments. The increased inmate load also contributed to over crowding and double cell assignments.

When we were building the replacement federal prison camp, a large number of bunk bed units were received from several military bases. Right away we noticed a problem with the bunk beds. The tops and bottom of each corner post had a 40mm grenade launcher shell casing mounted on each bunk. It is against federal law for felons to have access to the brass so staff removed the shell casings from the more than 400 bunk bed units.

At the penitentiary new bunks were received from military surplus. The bunks were assembled by the federal camp inmates and staff brought in the several hundred bunk bed units and stored them just outside the work corridor of the penitentiary.

There were a couple of problems with that arrangement. The first problem was the bunks were assembled and could not be placed in the cells. The bunks were at least 30 inches wide and the cell doors were about 28 inches wide. A fully assembled bunk would not go through the cell door.

The second problem was the metal bracing on the bunks were ready made "Shanks" and swords. The metal could sharpen quite easily into a weapon that could be used by the inmates. The bunks had to be taken apart, moved into the cell blocks, reassembled and welded together inside the cells. I think the bunk count was 800 or 900 bunks to be installed. This was a very large job.

One problem that was an ongoing concern was the outside window cell bars. The bars could be cut through or twisted with a tool called a "Bar Breaker." A constant check of the bars was made by staff. This process was called "Bar taps."

A few correctional officers used to perform bar taps during Sunday morning's rather than waiting until later in the week. They did this in order to wake up the inmates sleeping late.

Each week every steel bar in the unit had to be checked. Later heavy duty round stainless steel pipes and steel mesh covered the windows. The barriers still had to be checked. If I recall right, the pipes were concrete filled. When the steel mesh was installed, it ended the trash being thrown out the windows.

The prison cells are pretty small for two inmates. A cell measured only about 7 by 9 feet. The ceiling was 7 feet in height. In a double cell there was a combination toilet and sink, a writing table seat arrangement, two inmate lockers and double bunks were installed. This did not leave much room. No televisions were installed in the cells. I

In a general population unit there could be two televisions installed on the flats and a TV room with a TV set installed. For the most part inmates did not damage the TV sets. The subscription cable service was paid for from the inmate trust fund sales at the inmate commissary.

An ironing board would be installed in the unit and an electric iron was issued by the officer to an inmate for its use to iron clothes. There was at least one washing machine and dryer installed in a unit. Most units would have two.

Unit's generally had one common shower on each tier. The showers later had stainless steel walls installed to improve sanitation. There was a sink room for the orderlies to keep mops and mop buckets in. A staff restroom was available for the correctional officer. The unit team office was accessible from the unit.

Units would be repainted on a regular basis. Inmates could be issued paint brushes, paint rollers, and paint of selected colors that they could paint their assigned cells with.

WALKING MAINLINE

The federal prison camp had common showers, rest rooms, and open bay's for inmate bunk beds. The camp also had a laundry room for inmate use.

Chapter 26

INMATE WORK ASSIGNMENTS

The inmate work day starts at 7:40 A.M. work call and ends at 3:40 P.M. work recall for most inmates. The work week was Monday through Friday except for federal holidays and weekends.

All inmates in the system have a work assignment. The assignments vary institution to institution. Some of the assignments are very common, such as an orderly assignment, food service, recreation, A&O, unassigned, or other assignments.

Inmates were assigned to work details by the unit team. Most of the time it was the correctional counselor who made the SENTRY work assignments.

The A&O/UNICOR correctional counselor made the assignments to the federal prison industry jobs.

Inmates also had jobs in mechanical services. Some of those jobs were skilled labor jobs. Jobs like electrician, plumber, carpenter, and when we had the machine shop, an inmate machinist.

There were certain inmate job assignments, in prison industries, that had an inmate designated as a leadman assignment. The inmate would be like a foreman of a crew. The job was to insure the production goals of the group was met. Inmates were not supposed to be in a position to supervise other inmates.

In food service for example you had inmate assignments, such as, trash dock, the bakery, or the pots and pans crew.

195

There were cook crews, clean up crews, and a crew that would be issued knives and worked locked in secure area where carving and cutting of meat took place.

Unit's had unit orderly crews. An inmate orderly was responsible for cleaning the housing units. Education had inmates assigned as tutors, law library clerks, and orderlies.

The UNICOR jobs were in the cable factory, sign factory, print plant, business office, and the UNICOR maintenance crew.

The recreation department had inmates who worked the recreation yard or gym orderly crew.

The safety department had inmates who worked in that office.

Laundry had inmates who issued inmate clothing, operated the washing machines, and the supply room.

The hobby shop inmates were assigned for cleaning and hobby shop operations.

The chapel had an inmate crew to clean and help in the maintenance of the chapel.

Inmates who refused a work assignment were placed in administrative detention, also known as "the hole."

The federal prison camp had similar work crews as the penitentiary with additional assignments of the fire department crew, beef cattle crew, farm crew, dairy cattle crew, outside landscape, power house, and sewage treatment plant crew.

There was a Vandenberg Air force assignment that provided landscape maintenance support to the base. For some inmates this was a great work assignment to be on, it was time away from the prison camp, working in the outdoors with plenty of fresh air.

There was a inmate assignment driving 18 wheel trucks for delivery of dairy and meat products to other federal prisons in the western region. For an inmate who was a licensed commercial truck driver, this was another great work assignment.

For a few inmates at the federal prison camp, the camp offered too much freedom and they ended up being transferred to a higher security prison.

Chapter 27

MISCONDUCT

This chapter has to deal with staff actions more than anything else. For the most part staff are: honest, reliable, and do what they are required to do. A few staff will go out of their way to take actions that are against policy, wrong and illegal.

When staff are caught, arrested, or prosecuted for criminal acts that take place in the prison, it is a very sad day.

One of my first times working with the special investigative supervisor (S.I.S.), who is like the internal affairs of a police department, was when I was working morning watch in 4 tower. Tower 4 was the rear sally port control tower. During the day shift that tower officer was responsible for vehicles and staff entry into the prison. The tower controlled the large 20 foot high steel gates that would open and close to allow vehicles to enter and leave the prison.

I was called on the telephone one morning at about 7:00 A.M.. The S.I.S. lieutenant asked me if a certain staff member entered the rear sally port yet. The staff member had not arrived for work at that time. It was common for some staff to enter through the rear entrance and report to work.

I was instructed to call a telephone extension and inform the person who answered the phone the staff member was in the rear sally port. The instructions were to tell the staff member the personnel gate was having problems and to have the staff member wait inside the sally port.

The personnel gates were in fine working order. About 30 minutes later that staff member was at the rear personnel gate.

He was carrying a large ice chest type container for his lunch, which was his custom. I let him into the sally port, informed him over the public address system the inner personnel gate was not working right and the security officer was coming out to repair it. He was told to have a seat inside the sally port.

The phone number was dialed, person who answered the phone was told the staff member had arrived and was in the sally port.

About a minute later several cars arrived at the base of the tower, FBI Agents, DEA Agents, a Deputy US Marshal, and the S.I.S. lieutenant got out of the cars and entered the rear sally port. The staff member was arrested. His lunch chest was searched and several pounds of marijuana were found. The staff member was placed in the back of one of the FBI agent's cars and all the vehicles left.

The tower relief arrived at the end of the morning watch shift and asked how the shift went. He was told it was quiet and routine. The tower log book indicated otherwise.

One morning I had arrived a few minutes earlier than normal and parked the car in the staff parking lot. Our resident FBI agent met me and asked me to wait a few minutes out in the parking lot. That statement made my heart skip a few beats.

The FBI agent then started to tell me about a food service cook foreman and how he had known his father for years. He said that he had seen the food service cook foreman grow up, go to school, and got his first job with the bureau of prisons. He said the food service foreman did not know what was going to happen to him next.

The FBI agent pointed out two other FBI agents waiting inside the fence on the other side of the main entrance sally port. He told me it was a sad day for him.

We watched the food service cook foreman get out of his car, go to the trunk and retrieve a package from it. He then went into the prison. The food service foreman was met in the front lobby entrance by FBI agents who placed him into hand cuffs and walked him out of the prison to an agent's car.

The FBI agent that met me in the parking lot, told me it was okay to report to work, and word would spread about what had happened that morning. I reported to work and went to my assigned post for the day.

I used to worry about being set up by inmates. I rented a post office mail box for my mailing address. It was something I did from my army days in the 1970's. It was easier to have a post office box address rather than changing the address every time I moved.

I worried about getting an unsolicited package filled with drugs or an envelope filled with money at my post office box. It would be easy to set someone up this way.

There was a staff member who worked in the laundry as a foreman. He had a mail box just a few rows down from me at the local post office. He would retrieve a package or two on a regular basis from his mail box.

The postal service leaves a notice in your mail box if the package is too big to fit in the mail box. You take the card and give it to the counter person and they will get your package for you. I used to order books and other merchandise by mail order. I was at the post office on a day off to get mail. The staff member who worked in the laundry room was there also. He had picked up a package from the front counter staff and went out the door to the parking lot.

When he left, I saw what looked like a surveillance team follow him. He was on the way to the prison. I figured it was none of my business and did not think much of it.

After my two days off when I reported for work I learned he had been arrested by the US Postal Inspectors and the FBI. He had been taking drugs into the prison.

When I was assigned as the control room officer, I talked with a unit officer who remarked he was just like the inmates in the prison. The statement was a puzzle to me until one evening shift.

After normal business hours the control room officer answers the telephone for the prison. Every once in a while, staff place a collect phone to the prison. Most of the time it was a prank, something to annoy the control room officer with and be a waste of time.

It was during the first part of an evening watch shift I received a collect telephone call from the same officer who had said he was just like the inmates. He was calling from a local county jail. He said he was arrested for bank robbery and would not be able to report for his next work shift. I passed the call to the operations lieutenant.

It was during one evening shift the control room officer called for all available staff to report to control. This was a very unusual call. Staff responded quickly to the control room.

The warden and executive staff were all present. Staff were ordered to form a line on both sides of the corridor, evenly spaced, from the control room along the west corridor, to the hobby shop.

A few minutes later, the hobby shop supervisor, who was a staff member, was lead down the corridor in handcuffs, and escorted out the control room sally port. He was under arrest.

Later I had to identify inmates on the video tape who were with the staff member when he was cutting and distributing marijuana. One of the inmates looked very nervous and concerned. He was an inmate on my correctional counselor case load. The staff member was sentenced to do prison time.

When I was assigned as a computer specialist, we had a staff member who was working as the carpenter shop foreman. He had stated he had sympathy toward a prison gang and wanted to be a member of that gang.

The problem with that is, a correctional officer cannot cross the line, even though you want to be a prison gang member, you can never be because of being an officer. A corrupt officer is looked at as a pretty low life. He ended up doing prison time.

There was a correctional officer who made the local newspapers and television news when he was busted in a shopping center parking lot delivering drugs to an undercover agent.

Chapter 28

NICKNAMES

Nicknames are used to hide the identity of the inmate. Nicknames could be the street name of the inmate. There are many more reasons for inmate nicknames.

A few inmates were known from the area they lived. "Pico," was an inmate from Pico Rivera California. "Tony Pro," was a famous individual from the New York City area. "Puppet," was an inmate on my case load who was killed at the prison. "Hollywood," was an inmate who was assaulted by an inmate nicknamed "Turtle." When staff responded to the call for assistance "Hollywood," had taken away the weapon that "Turtle," tried to use to kill him. Turtle was being beaten up by "Hollywood," over the assault.

"Baby Ray," "Stick Em Steve," "Air Vernon," and "Taco," were a few more inmates. "Taco," liked to tickle a person's ribs for some reason. The person he did this too felt like their ribs were broken or very sore afterwards.

"The Snake," was a very famous inmate who tended to a rose garden in the prison recreation yard.

"Snitch," "Cheese Eater," "Leg Rider," and "Rat," were a few terms used both for staff and inmates. It was best not to have those terms as a nickname.

It was one of the duties of staff to note the nicknames of inmates they worked with on the crew they supervised. Inmates would come to the door of a housing unit and call for an inmate by his nickname. An effort was made to document the information.

Many times during a mass interview of inmates in a unit, inmates would not know the name of an assault victim, but when a photograph of the inmate was shown they knew the inmate by a nickname. This information helped in the investigation.

The nickname "Fish," is applied to new inmates to the prison system and to new staff. The description "A fish out of water," could describe the behavior of both inmates and staff in a penitentiary environment when they first arrive.

Officer "Vah-Cot–Tea," was famous for working many a shift on the correctional services roster when the post could not be filled.

"Five-O," was a nickname for correctional workers and was used as a warning when staff were walking the unit. "Man Walking," was a term used also. "Hack," "Turn Key," "Boss," "Screw," and some other names were used to describe correctional officers.

The term "Guard," was used many times to describe correctional staff. This is not a correct term. All staff in the prison are sworn federal law enforcement officers. Some staff have the primary job of "correctional officer." All staff are correctional workers and the first duty is the correctional role. Not all states recognize federal law enforcement as "Peace Officers," the term "Peace Officer," is subject to state law.

Staff members sometimes would get nicknames for various reasons. We had a staff member whose nickname was "Pumpkin Head." There was another staff member who was known as "Buck Shot." "Boom Boom," would be added to the staff member's name if they had an accidental discharge of a firearm in one of the prison's towers.

"Slam Dunk," was given to a correctional officer who was responsible for having a large number of inmates both placed in detention and being prosecuted for federal crimes within the prison.

"Fore Skin," was the name of a control room officer who later became a correctional counselor. "Howdy Doody," was a nickname for a case manager who looked like the puppet that was on television in the 1950's. "Pretty Boy," was a correctional officer whose claim to fame was his hair. "Slime Boy," was a correctional officer whom inmates liked to fill a plastic honey bear containers with urine and feces and spray the fluid on. "Nacho," was a staff member in the education department. "Chicken Bob," was staff member who was well known at the prison.

"CB," was the voice of Lompoc penitentiary. His voice was the greeting on the automated telephone system. He worked custody for years and became a correctional counselor. He transferred to another BOP facility and retired.

"Special K," was a correctional officer who would write extensive amounts of information on the back of an inmate's 5x8 housing card. He knew his inmates. He later was selected as a correctional counselor and retired from the bureau.

"Chilly Willy," was a correctional supervisor. "Buck," was a correctional supervisor who had no body hair.

There were some wardens who had nicknames. "Chilly Bob," and "Fat Pat," come to mind. "Short Tie," was an executive staff member.

Chapter 29

RECREATION YARD

The recreation yard is a great place to go just to get the fresh air and be in the open. In 1985 the weight pile was a place where inmates were able to work out frustrations and anger. It was true quite a few inmates bulked up and gained muscle and strength.

To me, having to take an inmate to the ground, who had a lot of muscle that limited his mobility was easier than having to fight with an inmate who was limber. Either way, it was by choice of the inmate and how he was acting if he had to be taken to the ground. It was up to how the inmate was behaving.

During the years when Lompoc was a penitentiary, many times staff responded to fights on the recreation yard.

Problems on the recreation yard could develop very rapidly. A few times an inmate would run for the fence in an escape attempt or even "Suicide by Cop." Riots could occur, and an assault, or killing would happen.

Most of the time inmates did not cause any problems on the yard. The recreation yard was a place inmates could conduct business and not be readily overheard by staff. The normal number of staff assigned to the yard itself was low. The running track was a place where inmates could walk or run. This was an open area with a strong ocean breeze.

Softball was played inside the fence, along with handball, and bocce ball. There was a building on the yard where recreational equipment was issued to the inmates.

The warden did approve of a rodeo complete with bucking horses and bull riding. That is an event that was different and took a lot of organizing to put the rodeo on.

Sometimes staff who had disagreed with the prison executive staff would be placed on duty in the recreation yard. The duty hours were from 6:00 A.M. to 2:00 P.M. and generally there was no extra pay, just the ordinary day watch base pay. All that was expected of the staff was to watch the inmates.

Congress had passed a law that the weight piles were not going to be allowed in federal prisons. Our warden at the time had informed the inmates he would allow the weight pile to stay if there was not any trouble on the yard. He informed the inmates the first sign of trouble or any problems happening on the recreation yard the weights would be gone.

A few weeks later there was an incident on the recreation yard. The prison was locked down and overnight the weight pile was gone.

The warden ordered trucks and fork lifts to come into the recreation yard and remove the weight pile. All that was left was a cement pad where the weight pile was. Congress should let the prison system executives and staff run the prison system, and not interfere with prison operations

Out at the federal prison camp there was a full size, professional base ball field. The inmates had also built a high quality bocce ball court.

When there was bad weather and in the evening hours the indoor gym was available. The movie theater was part of the recreation department.

WALKING MAINLINE

The movie theater was always a difficult post for a correctional officer. There could be up to 300 inmates in the theater and one officer. It was very difficult to monitor inmate behavior and if there was a problem about the only thing the officer could do was call for assistance.

An inmate work crew was assigned to mow the grass and perform clean up on the recreation yard. The work was not very hard. One of the Mafia bosses maintained a rose garden in the recreational yard.

There were a large number of gopher and ground squirrel holes in the recreation yard. A few times those holes would cause an inmate or staff member to trip and fall. When this happened the armed patrol or tower officer would be on a higher level of alert insuring the person was not an assault victim.

Chapter 30

RELIGION

The penitentiary at Lompoc had Protestant, Catholic, and Muslim chaplains. The penitentiary also had an outside rabbi visit on a regular basis. The religious practices of the American Indian were recognized. The medicine bag that an American Indian wore around his neck was a religious object and subject to search by the chaplain.

The first warden I worked for had banned the wearing of head gear in the chow hall. The case was taken to court since the Indians wanted to wear head bands. The warden's banning of head gear was upheld by the court. Unless an inmate was working the food line or where health standards required some type of head gear no hats or any type of head gear was worn by inmates in the dining room.

Outside guests and volunteers were allowed to visit the prison and conduct religious services. When the prison was in lock down status the outside visitors and volunteers were not allowed inside.

The federal prison camp had some of the same guests and volunteers as the penitentiary. The Nation of Islam was also recognized and allowed to have most of their beliefs be practiced in the prison.

All the volunteers and outside visitors had to be cleared by national level and other law enforcement agency checks. This process could be a one time check or allow regular access up to a year at a time.

Inmates could get married to a woman on the outside after undergoing a long administrative process. The marriage could not be consummated while the inmate was incarcerated. At the prison there were no conjugal visits.

As a correctional officer, I would escort outside volunteers and visitors for the religious services department when I was able. As a correctional counselor I was able to assist the department in the escort process and in the records checks when they would be needed. Part of my duties as a unit correctional counselor was to perform the records checks on inmate visitors. I was trained and certified to do the work. This just made things go more smoothly for the prison.

Since a series of court decisions in the 1960s and 1970s, the constitutional right of prisoners to practice religion has been widely recognized. Congress passed a federal law based on the rulings, recognizing prisoner religious rights known as the Religious Land Use and Institutionalized Persons Act of 2000. The most common right exercised is the right to attend religious services in various denominations. Not only are Christian religions represented, but prisoners have the right to worship Islam, Buddhism, and other recognized religions.

Some practices not considered part of an established organized religion are not allowed. Inmates can also observe special diets and possess religious items, such as prayer beads, feathers, medicine pouches, and prayer rugs, as long as they do not interfere with prison operations.

Which faith groups are active in a prison depend on the specific needs of its inmate population. Larger prisons often offer services in many different denominations on a daily basis. Smaller facilities may offer only nondenominational (not belonging to a particular religion) services held on Sundays, with smaller activities available a couple times a week.

Chapter 31

SANITATION

Prison sanitation was emphasized as a very high priority in the penitentiary. When you see a prison on television or in the movies you see dark, dank and dirty places. At Lompoc it was a very pleasant surprise on how clean and bright the penitentiary is. It still is a prison, the gray cement walls are there on the outside, but step into the main corridor the floor is highly polished and clean.

The main corridor is about 20 feet wide and 632 feet from the west end wall to the east end wall. Orderlies are assigned to make sure the place stays clean and not cluttered. From time to time there are changes to the paint colors on the doors, grills, and the walls. Considering how much inmate movement and foot traffic during the day it is a very clean place. The units are normally clean and orderly.

When and if a prison disturbance occurs, this is when you see the prison get trashed, flooded, and pretty much made a mess. That does not happen very often.

When I was still a correctional counselor during a lock down, I was assigned to work in "F" unit. Inmates were throwing trash out on the ranges and the tiers. I took plastic bags gave them to staff and told them to go to cell to cell and have the inmates put the trash in the bags. The bags were piled in a storeroom and removed twice a day to clean up the unit. It worked pretty well.

After our 4:00 P.M. count cleared an officer and I started to scrub the first floor of the unit. We could not let any inmates out for clean up, but to keep the staff busy we started the mopping and cleaning of the unit. After a couple of hours we got buffers out and started to polish the floors. The goal was the floors should be polished to the point of looking like an ice skating rink, and to really shine.

An associate warden came to visit the unit and he asked what the heck we were doing. He was informed we were getting the unit ready for late night TV inspection. We wanted the cleanest unit, he looked at us and just shook his head.

After the prison came off lock down, the associate warden arranged to have the unit get late night TV and to be called first for the recreation yard and for meal calls, all because we had kept the unit clean during a lock down. During the lock down other units were just trashed.

Every week the unit inmate orderly assigned to the job, would obtain cleaning supplies from our safety department. Quite a few times the unit would run low or run out of floor wax and other items for cleaning.

Certain staff were known to hoard supplies. Since I had been on a staff shake down crew, I knew of just about every hiding place or storage area in the prison.

I knew how to obtain these supplies without getting caught. Better yet I had a couple of hiding places that unless you knew them, were not an easy access to other staff. I did go out and procure what was needed to kept the unit clean, and what was needed for the orderlies to do their job.

During the time I was the "L" Lincoln unit correctional counselor, the unit was visited by the Director of the Bureau of Prisons. I had been told it was possible I could have a VIP visit and to have my unit ready for inspection.

WALKING MAINLINE

We did not have any liquid cleaning supplies, no floor wax, not anything and was not able to get any. We had mops, mop buckets, pails, a few brushes, a high speed buffer and two regular floor buffers. The unit had an inmate orderly crew of 15. They were told everyone had to be working, buffing the floor, cleaning the showers and the unit. They were to make the unit look good. The crew all said okay and started to work.

The director, our warden, associate wardens, executive staff, and the unit manager all came to visit about 9:30 A.M.. The inmates were working, three buffers were being operated on the first floor, inmates were mopping and cleaning the showers. It looked like a very busy crew.

The director was very pleased, saying we were a very productive unit, we were making good use of the inmates time, and congratulated the unit manager. The associate warden was very happy.

After the director left the unit all the inmates on the crew asked how the visit went, and they were told very good. The unit did get first call for meals, recreation yard or the gym, and late night TV privilege for over a week.

Before the mesh screening was placed over the unit windows there was a trash problem on the outside of the housing units. A grounds crew was to clean this outside trash. For a long time unit management had an associate warden who delighted in selecting certain correctional counselors to take an inmate orderly crew outside of the prison walls but inside the prison fence to pick up this trash.

My unit and crew would be selected on a very regular basis. This was done sometimes because certain unit team staff would anger the associate warden. Trash pick up was not a real pleasant experience.

One weekend the case manager and I were supervising a cleaning detail outside the east end housing units. We had the crew in front of the corner gun tower. The inmates were told if they found contraband to point it out to the staff supervising them. Let staff recover the contraband.

That day one of the inmates had found a prison made knife on the ground. It was about a 12 inches long. The inmate had picked the knife up and was poking it lightly into the back of the case manager trying to gain his attention.

The tower officer had observed the inmate picking up the knife and had drawn his weapon to fire at the inmate. The armed patrol vehicle was getting into position to provide cover fire if needed. The officers could not get a clear shot because the case manager and I were in the line of fire.

I turned around, saw the inmate with the knife, I took the knife from the inmate and told him "Don't do that!" The inmate was told the tower officer would shoot him because he would not know what was going on. This could have been a problem for the inmate.

Another time I had taken the crew between "J" unit and the laundry room of the prison. There was a family of cats and kittens living under the stair steps. There were about a dozen cats and they were all wild. The kittens were just coming out from under those steps.

The inmate crew of six inmates and I were getting too close to the kittens. The wild cats started to hiss and arch their backs at us. Several of the adult cats began to chase after us.

I did what could have been a stupid thing, I told the inmates to run and follow me around the end of the unit. A chain link fence divided the area in half and the fence ran to the base of the gun tower from the corner of the unit.

I was running around the corner with six inmates following me being chased by cats. The gun tower officer seeing all this jumped to his feet with his high-powered rifle ready to fire. I was at the fence gate opening it for the inmates to go through.

The cats had formed a line and sat down a few feet from us. I told the tower officer on the radio we were avoiding the cats. He responded he could see that now. It was not one of my smartest moves and the situation could have been tragic.

Chapter 32

SPECIAL HOUSING

The special housing unit (SHU) was also known as the "Hole." It is the cell block that inmates were locked in their cells 23 hours a day. Before the inmates are let out of the cells they are placed in restraints.

The unit housing cell assignments would be divided into administrative detention, disciplinary segregation, protective custody, and special cases.

The US Marshal Holdover unit was a special housing unit where inmates awaiting assignment and movement by the US Marshal Service were placed. This was also a lock down unit.

Administrative detention is non punitive in nature. Disciplinary segregation requires a 30 day review of the inmate.

Visiting a special housing unit as a staff member can be an experience. The entrance into the unit is of the sally port style. That is when the outer door is open the inner door is secured.

Staff members who are not assigned to the unit sign the visitor log book. Prison keys are secured in a locked box before entry into the unit. Inmate orderlies are allowed out of their cell to work on the range when the other inmates are secured in the cells and staff are not on the range.

Staffing levels are higher in the unit since there is a need for more correctional staff to work the unit. Officers escort inmates to the recreation cages, showers, visits, disciplinary hearings, hospital trips, and so on.

A correctional officer monitors the inmates while they are in the recreation cages. A correctional officer has to open and close cell doors, and issue razors to inmates taking showers. The inmates have to be fed three meals a day and the meals are served by staff. It is a labor intensive process.

The officer in charge maintains the record books and logs that document meals, showers, recreation, medical care, and other entries required by policy. Those records are filed in the inmate's central file.

Staff members are subject to assaults by inmates. Sometimes an inmate may fix a mixture of urine and feces in a container to throw on a staff member.

Sometimes a forced cell move is ordered. A forced cell move is an action that is used when an inmate has become so assaultive or disruptive he has to be placed in four point restraints. When this happens, the inmate gets checked on a regular basis to insure he has not injured himself, evaluate his mental condition, and to see if he has calmed down.

Working in a special housing unit is very busy and time goes pretty fast for staff. For an inmate locked in a cell, the time goes very slow. A protective custody case can be pretty demanding and many times extra precautions have to be made to insure the inmate's safety.

A few times an inmate may get mad and start flooding his cell. He may plug the toilet or sink and run the water until the water runs out the cell on to the tier. This flooding can cause a mess in other inmate cells and cause slip and fall injuries to staff. The water has to be turned off to the cell and the SHU staff members have to deal with the inmate.

Working the tier as an officer you went and cuffed the inmates, escorted them to the recreation cages, to the showers, to visiting, to the disciplinary hearings, or other locations outside the cell. This is a time both the officer and the inmate are most vulnerable for an assault. A few times an inmate's cell partner would wait for his cell mate to be placed in restrains and he would attack the inmate.

A few times when inmates were not placed in restrains properly they have assaulted staff. In a special housing unit of the bureau of prisons more than one time an officer has been killed by an inmate. The highest rates of inmate assaults on staff happen most often in the special housing units.

Inmates are allowed shower time. During this time a razor is issued and must be retrieved from the inmates before they return to their cells. A few times when staff are busy, a razor has been known to be kept by the inmates and used in an assault.

The morning watch officer in charge of a special housing unit has to type up the reports and has to make sure all the documentation on the inmates is current and up to date. The board shows cell assignments, separation assignments, and other inmate status has to be current. It is a busy time and the job has to be performed correctly.

Clothing exchange, bedding exchange and just everyday housekeeping is more intense in the special housing units.

Unit team staff, the unit manager, case manager, and correctional counselor, make weekly rounds to see all the inmates on their case load. Executive staff make rounds in the special housing units on a regular basis. The institutional duty officer also makes regular visits. The correctional shift supervisor monitors the unit's on a daily basis.

Inmates can be very demanding and file law suits in federal court while in a special housing unit. Most of the time before an inmate can file a case in federal court the administrative remedy system must be exhausted. Informal resolution of a problem is attempted and if that is not successful, then the written process may be started at the local level. If the inmate is not satisfied with the local process, he can take the appeal to the regional office. If the appeal is not resolved at the region, it maybe filed with the central office in Washington, D.C..

The administrative remedy process is in place to allow an inmate to file his complaint and obtain a resolution to a problem. A few inmates are known as "filers," abuse the system as much as they can just to have something to do.

Chapter 33

SUICIDE

Suicide (Latin suicidium, from sui caedere, "to kill oneself") is the act of a human being intentionally causing his or her own death. Suicide is often committed out of despair, or attributed to some underlying mental disorder which includes depression, bipolar disorder, schizophrenia, alcoholism, and drug abuse. Financial difficulties, interpersonal relationships and other undesirable situations play a significant role.

In the prison environment an inmate may want to commit suicide when they are first placed in prison. In federal court a person could be convicted and taken directly to a federal prison.

This comes as a shock to an individual who thought they were going to be found not guilty in court or at sentencing. A few times I saw inmates come off the bus still in the street clothes and they could not believe they were being locked up in a penitentiary. This can lead to a suicide attempt.

One of my first dealings with an inmate who said he was going to kill himself was in our lower "I" unit. The inmate was in what was called box car cells. I was escorting the physician assistant on his rounds and we stopped to examine an inmate who had said he wanted to commit suicide. He really did not give a reason.

The old time physician assistant explained to the inmate on exactly how he should cut himself in order to bleed to death quickly. The method he described was such even if staff could respond or did respond in time the inmate would bleed to death.

The inmate became angry with us and asked if we were trying to kill him. The physician's assistant had told me the inmate was just acting out and did not really want to kill himself.

The physician's assistant also told me when an inmate did not say anything about killing himself or had changes in behavior from what was considered normal for that inmate, then it was time to watch out. He said some of the inmates wanted to play games or manipulate the system.

I was working in our US Marshal Holdover unit when I had an inmate that played the suicide game. He was faking attempted suicide. He would drink mixtures of cigarette ashes and torn up cigarettes to make him sick and look like he was killing himself. He would at times fall to the floor, pretending to be dying.

The inmates on the tier would yell "Man Down," and this brought a response from the unit officers. At times during count the inmate would be faking being suicidal, you could watch his eyes follow you when you walked past the cell he was housed. He would pretend to be passed out.

One afternoon he had taken shoe laces from a pair of military boots and tied a noose with a slip knot at the end of the laces. He then put one end through an air vent grate and the other around his neck. He was standing on the edge of a stainless steel toilet and said he was going to hang him self.

We requested the staff psychologist to respond to the inmate. While the psychologist was responding to the unit, the inmate slipped on the edge of the toilet and fell. The shoestring tightened around his neck and he choked to death. The forensic psychological examination concluded the death was accidental.

The prison used to have trained inmate suicide monitors who were stationed on the second floor of our hospital unit when an inmate was placed on suicide watch. The monitor was part of the peer treatment group. It was thought an inmate who wanted to kill himself could deal better with a fellow inmate rather than with a staff member.

An inmate who was placed on suicide watch would be in a strip cell. The inmate would be allowed to wear shorts and nothing else. The cell would have as little furnishings as possible so an inmate could not use anything to harm himself.

This program was discontinued and staff would be posted instead. This assignment was not the most pleasant to work. During the times I worked the post, I did not have an inmate complete a suicide.

All staff received some training concerning the signs of possible suicidal behavior. When an inmate is first committed to prison, this is a time that is a high stressor and could lead to a possible suicide attempt. Bad news such as a death in a family, or unfavorable ruling in a court case, drug use and other factors could lead to a suicide. Changes in behavior could be a sign an inmate has made up his mind to kill himself. Those stressors can apply to staff also.

I worked with a correctional officer who was on the fast track to becoming a lieutenant. It was a job he really wanted. He had a perfect work record until one day he did not show for his shift.

The operations lieutenant wrote him down as AWOL (absent without leave). He was AWOL for three days. I heard about this and ask his fellow co-workers if they had talked with him or had any contact with him. I checked with the operations lieutenant to see if any telephone calls were made to see if the officer was having any problems. I was told no attempt was made to contact the officer and none of his co-workers had talked with him. I went to the captain and asked if anyone knew where the officer lived and did anyone go check on the officer. Up until this point no one had.

One of the lieutenants went to the officer's apartment complex to check on the officer. The apartment manager was contacted and had keys to the officer's apartment. When the apartment was entered the officer was found in his bed.

He died of a self inflicted 9mm gunshot wound. Later we learned he had a breakup with his girlfriend. As far as anyone could determine this may have been the reason why he committed suicide.

Correctional counselors are provided extensive suicide prevention training. It is part of the certification process to be a trained counselor. Having the training helps prevent suicides but not always. An inmate can make up his mind to commit suicide and not much can be done about it.

An inmate on my case load worked out in the sign factory. He was showing signs of depression and having personal problems he would not discuss. I had talked with his supervisor and the unit officer.

Contact was made with the prison chaplain about the inmate. One day during work and tool call the inmate took an electrical extension cord, wrapped it around his neck, and hung himself. Responding staff tried to save the inmate but he died.

The term successful suicide was used to describe when an inmate killed himself. During our training we were told the correct term was completed suicide not attempted.

Over at the Federal Correctional Institution just after it was converted from a prison camp to a higher level prison an inmate jumped off the roof to his death on the front steps of a dormitory building.

Staff do look for signs and indicators of suicidal behavior. It is not always possible to stop an inmate who wants to kill himself.

Chapter 34

TELEPHONE CALLS

Inmates who wanted to place telephone calls in the prison on the inmate telephone system had to sign a consent to monitor form when they first processed into the prison. If the inmate refused to sign the form, then he would not be able to place telephone calls from the prison.

Inmate telephone calls were monitored and recorded. One of my assignments was as the telephone monitor. To me it was a job that required a lot of knowledge of the inmates. Certain inmates would have telephone restrictions and it was the job of the telephone monitor to insure the inmate did not make telephone calls during the restriction. After a while it became fairly easy to determine who was who on the telephone. The telephone monitor would hear the inmate on the telephone trying to place a phone call.

A phone call would be placed to the unit officer who would confirm a certain inmate was actually on the phone. The inmate could receive an incident report and be restricted to a longer time or some other disciplinary action could be taken. A few times because of the inmate abusing the telephone system he could be placed in the "Hole," or even charged with a criminal act and taken to federal court.

Most of the time the telephone monitor would be pulled to stand steam line, perform shakedown duties, or some other correctional officer assignment.

After a while the gun towers were wired to monitor inmate telephone calls. The number of inmate telephones available in a housing unit ranged from one to at least three telephones. This provided more staff coverage to monitor inmate telephone calls.

In the special housing units an inmate telephone was mounted on a cart would be wheeled from cell to cell. An inmate who was not on a telephone restriction list could place a collect telephone call from this phone.

Chapter 35

TRAINING

The Bureau of Prisons provides a lot of training to staff. The training can take place at the Staff Training Academy in Glynco Georgia, Staff Training Center Aurora Colorado, at the institution, or other locations. The training officer at the institution is the key staff member to help staff in choosing a training program.

Computer-based training was being introduced before I retired from the bureau. Before that paper-based training was the normal method of delivery of the information. Testing and certification was provided by the training officer.

Annual Refresher Training, (A.R.T.) was a requirement of all staff. This one week classroom based training was generally held outside the prison at the our staff training center. The uniform was civilian clothing. The training officer is extremely busy during this time. The instructors have to show up at the scheduled time for the required classes. Firearms and self defense training is provided.

The training officer also insures institutional familiarization classes are scheduled for all new staff. This training is completed before the staff member is sent to the staff training academy in Georgia.

During the career of an employee many types of training is offered. Core skills is a course of training for middle management. The department heads and other select staff learn the policy and procedures of performing the job supervising staff and how to document both good and bad performance. The class is a lively class with both hands on training, lecture, and automated training. It was a very good class.

When I was first assigned to computer services one of the requirements of the position was going on a program review of another institution's computer services department. The review is an audit of the practices and procedures that policy dictates on how a department is supposed to comply with all the rules and regulations.

For some of the computer department heads it is a high stress time. Very few people like to have their work examined in great detail and have mistakes documented. The warden is provided an exit report on the results of the review. The general policy is the reviewer in charge delivers the report and the team leaves the institution immediately.

One course of training I did not attend was bus crew training. I was not inclined when I was a correctional officer to travel on a bus transporting inmates. I know many of my co-workers could not wait to attend the class.

I did complete armed escort training. This was a class where training was provided on how to transport inmates on local medical trips, escorted trips to other locations, and if allowed to funerals. The course was intense, hands on training, use of force training with a lot of time on the firearms range. Once you completed the training every year after you had to qualify on the advanced firearms course.

Central Inmate Monitoring was a required training course for correctional counselors, case managers, unit managers, lieutenants, and other staff involved with this program. In order to keep the job assignment you had to complete and pass the certification requirements.

Inmate discipline training was another course that was required for staff involved with the disciplinary process. The certification consisted of a live demonstration of holding the hearing and passing the written test. This was another must do training to remain employed.

Correctional counselors had to take training for suicide prevention and how to hold group counseling sessions.

I completed cross training in Prison Industries (UNICOR), Unit Management, Correctional Services, and Case Management. I decided I did not want to complete the practical exercise for the case management program which would have lead to certification as a case manager. When I was selected as a computer specialist, I was promoted to the same pay grade as a case manager.

I liked to say the Federal Bureau of Prisons had available the most training of any federal agency other than the military for its staff.

Chapter 36

WARDENS

One day before I retired, my boss and I were standing in the hallway outside of the Warden's office. This was a moment of reflection. I had worked under every warden on a long row of photographs of past wardens at the penitentiary.

A warden sets the tone of the operation for the prison. Each warden brings to a prison his style of leadership and how he views the operation, and the administration of the prison. The warden is the chief executive officer.

Wardens are selected by the director of the Bureau of Prisons with advice of an executive committee. The warden can make an institution or make a mess of the institution. I worked for all male wardens. It does not matter whether the warden is a male or female. The tradition was a penitentiary has male wardens assigned.

My first warden worked with the Director of the Bureau of Prisons. He was able to pick up the telephone and speak directly with the director about how Lompoc Penitentiary was going to be run. With this warden you knew exactly where you stood, and if you did wrong, to own up to it.

One of the members of the April fools class of 1985 became a warden before he retired. I expect he was a very good warden. The associate warden the computer services department was under became a deputy warden for him. I asked the associate warden before he transferred to work for my classmate, to tell him "Hello," from one of the class members of the April fools class 1985.

WALKING MAINLINE

We would have some really great wardens at Lompoc who understood how to be excellent leaders and were there during an emergency or crisis. They would let staff do the job.

We did have one warden that was "Walked out of the prison." He was relieved by a deputy director of the BOP. A major investigation was conducted. He did retire.

I liked my last warden. He rode horses and was a very good leader. The good warden's time goes way too fast. The wardens who were not so good, their time in charge seemed to go on forever.

To me what makes a good warden is a leader who allows staff to perform their jobs. The warden should not be a micro manager but they are to provide overall guidance on how the prison should be operated. Policy should not override good correctional judgment. The warden should provide the example of being firm, fair, and consistent.

The warden must have good public relations skills and an excellent working relationship with local law enforcement, news media and the public. Wardens give rewards when people do a good job. Staff should not fear speaking their mind to the warden. A good warden will listen to everyone, then select a course of action.

A warden should be able to adjust when things are not right. Wardens should allow staff to make mistakes and learn from the mistakes. A warden should be fair in having to punish staff when staff does wrong. Wardens need to have an open door. A warden should walk the tiers, work areas, staff offices, and be visible. Wardens are leaders.

The BOP being a quasi military organization, the warden is a commander of his prison or could be considered the captain of his ship. Being in command is not an easy job but it is very rewarding. There is really nothing to compare to this position.

Chapter 37

WORK ASSIGNMENTS

When I was A&O/UNICOR counselor, I had the Associate Warden ask me to create a work assignment for inmates called "Metal Detector." It sounds so simple to create a work position for an inmate. There is justification for the assignment. A memo was written for the Associate Warden's signature. The work assignment was entered into the SENTRY system.

There was the question on inmate pay. This was resolved because the money would come from the inmate funding of the UNICOR program. Pay was like 15 cents an hour or so.

The position was for inmates to work as orderlies cleaning the area around the metal detectors. The quota was for three inmates and we hired three inmates for the job.

Work assignments were generally performed by the unit team. All inmates had to have a work assignment. The unit counselor would assign inmates to various jobs in the prison except the UNICOR job assignments. This was the job of the A&O/UNICOR correctional counselor.

The A&O/UNICOR counselor controlled the waiting list for inmate assignments to the various factory jobs. The counselor also controlled the inmate assignments for the admission and orientation program.

The UNICOR waiting list was on a first come, first applied listing with adjustments for when an inmate was placed in the special housing unit, was released on a writ, or assigned to a UNICOR job.

WALKING MAINLINE

Each inmate that arrived to the prison was provided the opportunity to apply for a job in the prison factory system. The pay was good for inmates and the work was not that hard. Don't think inmate pay is very high, the pay rate was from $.23 to $1.15 per hour. The pay for an inmate orderly in a unit was like $.11 per hour or so for a paid position.

The inmate pay rate was not a very strong incentive, but if an inmate refused to work he would be placed in detention. The "Hole," was not a pleasant experience, locked in a cell 23 hours a day with about an hour of recreation or shower time allowed each day.

A work assignment to food service was not a high priority for most inmates. Working food service could mean having to get up at 3:00 A.M. and reporting for work in the chow hall. It could mean cleaning pots and pans and dumping leftovers. Food service was a seven days a week operation. Most of the inmates assigned to food service did get two days off for five days of work.

The jobs in mechanical services had their own benefits depending what an inmate could hustle and get away with.

Orderly assignments were pretty good for some inmates. Unit orderly assignment meant the inmate had a cleaning assignment in his unit and when finished he could obtain a pass from the unit officer to go to the recreation yard, education, or the general activities center when it was open.

Inmates can earn vacation time. After a year of working at a job assignment an inmate can earn a week's vacation time. The vacation is taken inside the prison. It is a time the inmate is not on a work assignment and is on vacation. A few inmates did take the vacation time and others just worked instead of taking the time off.

There were no rock piles for inmates to make big rocks into smaller rocks. Working hours were from 7:40 A.M. to 3:40 P.M. Monday through Friday except for federal holidays. Lunch was from 11:00 A.M. to 12:00 noon during the week and on weekends a brunch time was established.

Chapter 38

WALKING MAINLINE

The warden of the institution determines who walks the mainline. The term means being inside the prison, without an escort and have the freedom of movement or as much as you can have. This term also applies to outsiders without escort, and staff who work at the prison. Inmates who are designated for the prison and who are housed in general population are mainline. Very few outsiders ever walk the mainline without an escort.

We had a researcher who wrote a book about the prison. The book was a study of the prison and its culture. The warden at the time, had told the researcher if he was going to walk mainline he would have to undergo training just like staff.

He attended our staff training academy in Glynco Georgia just like any staff member. He was in the unique position of being able to be with staff members and not really be staff and have the ability to talk with the inmates and gain insights no staff member could obtain.

He responded to calls for assistance, killings, assaults, and any and all emergencies. His office was just off the main corridor of the penitentiary. He was also able to talk with the inmates and maintained the fine line of being a professional and not getting caught up with the inmate games.

When I read his book, it was very interesting. I knew of all the events in the book and even participated in much of the action. It takes a unique person to be able to see both sides of the story. It is vary hard not to be caught up in the culture either as a correctional worker or inmate. It was a daily test for him to keep it straight and in perspective.

Chapter 39

MISCELLANEOUS

This is the chapter that contains stories and events that do not fit in any other section of this book.

One of the first events I recall was about a lieutenant who was living on the reservation. Part of the story is a little fuzzy but this is what I recall.

I had worked with the lieutenant on several Witness Security transfer cases. He was authorized to carry and possess a 9mm semi-automatic pistol for use when performing this duty. One day apparently he was drinking to excess and decided to fire his weapon on the reservation housing grounds. This brought a response from staff.

Generally when a problem for the police occurred on the reservation grounds, even though the property was annexed by the City of Lompoc, the problem would be resolved with internal means.

The one part of the story that seems very creditable was the lieutenant had fired several rounds from his pistol when the warden decided to approach the man. The warden had thought the weapon was empty but the lieutenant demonstrated it was not. The situation was resolved. The lieutenant later retired from the BOP.

Every year there is a "Correctional Worker's Week," celebration. The event was generally during the month of May. Most of the time I would take my annual leave and be out of town. I would return to my hometown or even perform my military reserve duty. At the end of the week of celebration a pig roast would take place.

Sometimes some strange events could occur such as attendees standing around the barbecue pit and attempting to put out the fire by using natural bodily fluids that seem to occur after many beers are ingested.

Other times females would be asked to participate in certain judging contests consisting of what they would look like during a visual inspection of the skin. The contest would generally be involving the upper portion of the female body. Much of this would depend upon the amount of adult beverages that were consumed.

Our staff training center was a location for parties and sometimes just a plain old beer bust. Always if staff member drank too much transportation to their home was available.

There was an inmate writer who wanted to be compensated for his work for a large daily newspaper. According to the law and BOP policy an inmate cannot operate a business. He wanted to write for the outside newspaper for pay.

It was in June, 1988, a news article appeared in the paper stating the inmate, who wrote articles for the paper was placed in detention. After two days he was released. He wrote about prison conditions and how they could lead to a riot. He was critical of the warden.

A case was filed in federal district court concerning his transfer from the penitentiary. The court found that actions taken against the inmate were retaliatory but the court did stop the transfer of the inmate from Lompoc to another facility.

WALKING MAINLINE

On July 30, 1990, it was reported the nation's most famous "country club prison," was shutting down. The Lompoc Federal Prison Camp was being converted into a higher security federal prison. The replacement for the camp was a prison with fences and razor wire instead of small "off-limits" signs around the property.

The new prison would be where inmates had to wear khaki uniforms instead of shorts and T-shirts. This was to be a prison where inmates can't play tennis in the afternoon.

My assignment was the officer in charge of the Vandenberg inmate crew when the change over was made. On a Friday I had my last day being the supervisor of the crew. That Monday I returned to the penitentiary to work in "L" unit as the evening watch officer. I replaced the officer who was my friend and co-worker who later served time convicted of a federal firearm's charge.

It was on or about September 11, 1999, when an inmate, who was an orderly in my unit where I was assigned as correctional counselor, was given a pardon by the president of the united states and released from prison. He was one of the Puerto Rican nationalists doing time for conspiring to overthrow the U.S. government.

I knew an inmate that was convicted of being a spy against the Army Security Agency in Germany. He was in a housing unit I had worked. In my other life with the US Army he was pretty well known. He always told me he was not guilty of being a spy.

I was working as the Federal Prison Camp Officer in Charge (O.I.C.) during one evening shift. A staff member brought an inmate to the room next to camp control where our detention cell was.

The inmate was a mess, he was cut, bruised, his clothes were torn and dirty. He looked like he had been in a fight. I placed him into the detention cell and notified the hospital physician assistant to come and examine the inmate.

I took my camp patrol officer and conducted the 4:00 P.M. count. The day watch O.I.C. provided coverage for the inmate in the detention cell. The count cleared and I left the camp patrol officer to conduct the evening meal.

I returned to the camp control room to find out what had happened to the inmate. The inmate told me he fell in a cement mixer. I told him I have heard of inmates who were victims of assaults say they fell down the stairs, fell from the bunk, slipped in the shower, and a variety of other stories. I told the inmate falling into a cement mixer was a first.

At about that time the staff member supervisor of the work crew to whom the inmate was assigned arrived. He told me the crew was pouring cement from a large truck when he noticed the inmate was missing from the rear platform on the truck.

He had the truck operator shut down the mixer and he began to search for the inmate. Apparently the inmate had slipped on the platform and fell into the large cement mixer drum.

The staff member said all he could see was an arm sticking out of the drum. The inmate was pulled from the inside of the cement mixing drum. This was why he looked like he was in a fight. I asked the foreman to write a memo of what happened, and fill out an accident report.

Normally an inmate that was injured at work could receive an incident report for failing to follow safety instructions. In this case after the inmate was examined by the physician assistant, I released him to his prison camp quarters. The inmate did not need an incident report.

A few months later the inmate wanted to keep his clothes when he was released from custody as a souvenir of his close call. I wrote a memo to the warden requesting approval for the inmate to take his prison clothes with him when he was released. The warden approved the request. He also told the inmate not to fall into cement trucks in the future.

On occasion we would have to deal with intoxicated inmates. The federal prison camp inmates could smuggle real alcohol into the camp.

The inmates inside the penitentiary would make prison wine or "pruno" a really nasty and bad tasting stuff to drink.

I helped escort a camp inmate who was really drunk, he was pretty badly injured when he had tried to ride one of the dairy cows out on the prison dairy farm. The cow did not like having someone try to ride her and threw the wouldbe cowboy to the ground. The inmate did get a transfer to another higher level prison after he healed up from his injuries.

It was on a Thanksgiving day during my third year at the prison we were serving Cornish hens to the inmates in our hold over unit for the noon meal. I was kidding the inmates, we were serving the seagulls that normally were outside the units on a daily basis. This particular day the seagulls did not appear until after we had served the meal. It was strange the birds did not arrive until later in the day.

A few months after I was promoted to correctional counselor I was walking down the main corridor when I saw an officer struggling to handcuff an inmate. The inmate was going to be taken to the detention unit.

I stopped to assist the officer, in one swift move I had the inmate under control, placed the inmate in handcuffs, told the officer "Here you are," and released the inmate to the custody of the officer. The officer who later was promoted to a correctional counselor still reminds me of this event from time to time.

It was during a day shift one day the work corridor officer stopped an inmate carrying a package or a book. The officer opened the package to look at the contents. The package exploded, it was an improvised bomb. Staff responded to the incident. A new officer stopped the inmate who had carried the package placing the inmate in restraints.

Other staff escorted the injured officer to the prison hospital then to the local hospital in Lompoc for medical treatment. The concern was how injured was the officer. In hindsight it was kind of funny to see the officer covered with tiny pieces of paper that made it look like he was covered with chicken feathers.

I suppose in the weeks after the bomb blew up, it was not a really good thing to do in sneaking up on the officer and popping a paper bag filled with air behind his back.

The lesson learned is if an inmate is carrying a package, and staff want to examine what is inside, have the inmate open the package, and show the contents. In this case the inmate was attempting to place a bomb into an inmate's cell when the officer stopped him.

THE END

Prison terms and meanings as used in Lompoc Penitentiary

Admin detention: Administrative Detention. When a prisoner is placed admin detention he is being investigated and will be placed in a special housing unit the investigation is complete. See Segregation.

Beef: Criminal charges. Can also mean having a problem with someone.

Rec yard: Main recreation yard.

Bit: Prison sentence, example "I got a three-year bit."

Bitch, bitched out : sex partner, sex act.

Blocks: Cellhouses.

Books: Commissary account.

Bone Yard: Used to be the visiting patio in the penitentiary.

Bum Beef: A false accusation or wrongful conviction.

Call-out: Appointment.

Care Package: Money sent from a friend.

Catch a ride: Get high with someone.

The Chain: Used on the bus to secure prisoners.

Check-in: Protective Custody.

Convict : Old timers who live up to the convict code,

who aren't informants, who are loyal to the code, whose word is good, who won't play games.

Cop-out: Request to staff member.

Dis seg: Disciplinary Segregation.

Dummy Up: To shut up, to pipe down, to be quiet, especially about one's knowledge of a crime.

Fish: A new arrival, a first-timer, a bumpkin, not wise to prison life. New correctional officer.

Gate Money: The amount of money provided to an inmate when he is released from custody.

Gate Time: The time until release.

Hacks/Hogs/Pigs/Screws/Cops/Bulls: Correctional Officers.

Hold your mud: Not tell, even under pressure of punishment. Also used during a dry cell when an inmate does not have a bowel movement.

The Hole: Special Housing unit or segregation unit.

House: Cell.

Hustle: Any scheme to obtain money or drugs while in prison.

Inmate: A term for prisoners. Used by guards and administrators, or other inmates who are new to the system. Not a convict.

In the car: In on the "deal."

Iron Pile: Weights and weightlifting equipment.

Jacket: Prison central file containing all information on a prisoner. Also reputation.

Jigger: Lookout for staff.

Keister: To hide something in the rectal cavity, (pronounced keester).

Kite: Written correspondence.

Lame: Stupid or naive.

Lay-in: Sick or on vacation.

Lifer: Anyone with a life sentence.

Lock-down: When prisoners are confined to their cells.

Lock-up: Placed in a cell, sometimes P.C..

Lop: See inmate.

Main Line: Main population of the prison. Can also be used to refer to drug use.

Med-line: Medication line, pill-line, or pill call.

Mule: A person who smuggles drugs into the institution.

Old School: Old way of doing things, "he's an old school convict," meaning stand up.

On the leg: Trying to gain favors.

Paper: A small quantity of drugs packaged for selling. Dropping a note.

P.C.: Protective Custody.

Pruno: Homemade wine.

Punk: Homosexual or weak individual.

Rat/Snitch/Stool Pigeon: Informant.

Sallyport: Security entrance into the institution.

Scam: A scheme, hustle, or game.

Segregation : A disciplinary unit where prisoners are kept apart from the main population and locked down 23 hours a day.

Shake-down: Search.

Shank: Prison made knife.

Watch: Work shift for staff, also used when inmates are placed under direct observation.

Short: An inmate who is close to his release date.

Shot: Incident report.

Slammed: Locked in the hole.

Stash: To hide something.

Stand Point: Watch for "the man".

Stick: Stab.

Store: Commissary, some times inmates would run a store from the cell.

Turned out: Forced into homosexual acts. To "turn out" is to use someone for your own ends.

U.A.: Urinalysis.

www.ingramcontent.com/pod-product-compliance
Lightning Source LLC
Chambersburg PA
CBHW070155310326
41914CB00100B/1934/J